EYE SEE AMERICA
THROUGH THE LENS OF
JOSHUA MANN PAILET
October 2, 2010 - January 8, 2011

EXHIBITION SPONSORED BY

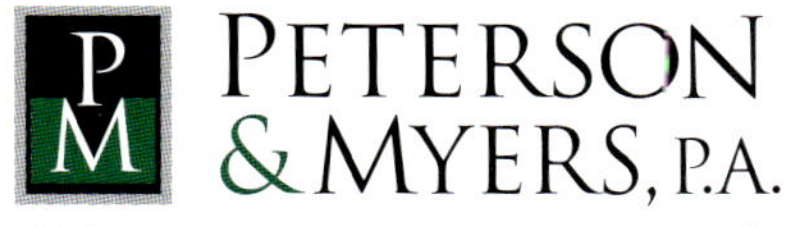

PETERSON
& MYERS, P.A.
ATTORNEYS AT LAW • SINCE 1948

and
Robert and Malena Puterbaugh

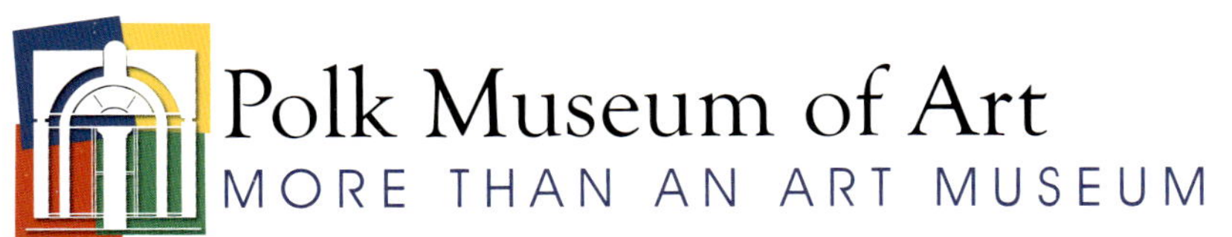

Polk Museum of Art
MORE THAN AN ART MUSEUM

ANNUAL EXHIBITION FUND SPONSORS:
Dorothy Chao Jenkins
The Reitzel Foundation
The Hazelle Paxson Morrison Foundation
BCI Engineers & Scientists

800 East Palmetto Street   Lakeland, Florida 33801-5529   T 863.688.7743   T 863.688.5423   WWW.POLKMUSEUMOFART.ORG

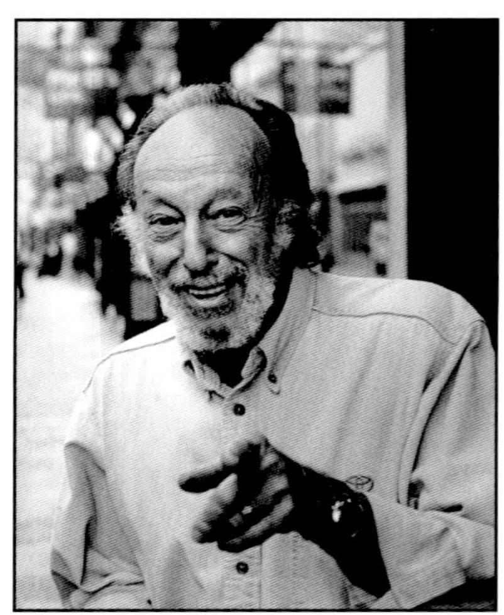

In Memory of
Herman Leonard
1923 - 2010

ACKNOWLEDGMENTS & PREFACE

by Daniel E. Stetson, Executive Director

Polk Museum of Art is honored to present this exhibition of work by New Orleans photographer Joshua Mann Pailet. Through this exhibition we celebrate Pailet's impressive talent, the legacy of fine art and documentary photography, and the compelling character of American culture.

So much of our understanding of our country and culture has been gained through photography. There is something distinctly American about documentary photography. Despite photography being a European invention, it has come to define American culture similar to Paris's historic relationship with painting. French born Henri Cartier-Bresson, Hungarian born André Kertész and Swiss born Robert Frank epitomized the documentary aesthetic and they all realized their vision, in part, by working in America. This is evidenced most directly in Frank's seminal production, *The Americans*, a photo essay and book.

Joshua pursued the documentary aesthetic and has distinctly made it his own over his four decades of making photographs. As Polk Museum of Art continues to emphasize the importance of contemporary American photography, we prize this exhibition as being one of our most definitive presentations. Joshua's photographs belong in the company of Gary Winogrand, Lee Friedlander and Robert Frank as documents from travels offering unique and telling views of America's character. Joshua's works present images of class differences, of human struggles and celebrations and he often uses a sly humor to point the way. He shows us contrasts and conflicts found on the street, in the auction houses and deep in the flood waters of Katrina. This is not just Woody Guthrie's and Jack Kerouac's America, it is Joshua's and all of ours.

It has been a great pleasure to work with Joshua and become better acquainted with his vast and beautiful oeuvre. From the initial conception of this exhibition, Joshua's knowledge of photography, and his ability to visually capture that knowledge so superbly in his own work, evidenced the exhibition's undeniable strength. Our anticipation has grown as we planned for the unveiling of this exhibition, its historic documentation through this catalogue, and the opportunity to introduce our audiences to the impressive visual aptitude of this great American photographer.

From his experiences on board the celebrated American Freedom Train in 1976 to his more recent portfolio of powerful images from the aftermath of Hurricane Katrina; from the electrifying energy he captures in his photographs of arena rock concerts, to his more intimate portraits from daily American occurrences; Pailet shares an evocative insight into his own, and our, American experience. This exhibition allows us to be much more than spectators; by viewing Pailet's photographs, we participate in the ongoing dialogue of American culture.

This exhibition and catalogue is the result of the kindness, generosity and determination of several very special people. First, I would like to extend a big thank you to this exhibition's lead corporate sponsor Peterson & Myers, P.A. for their generous support of this exhibition and the arts in general. Their sponsorship truly has made this project possible. I especially want to thank Bob and Malena Puterbaugh for their generosity and Bob for having been instrumental in realizing this project. They have given so much to help Polk Museum of Art preserve the legacy of fine art photography and build this center of excellence within our Permanent Collection. Bob's personal appreciation for photography is a moving force in seeing this exhibition into fruition; his enthusiasm for the arts is admirable and deeply appreciated. Our thanks also to David Ricketts of Fleetwing Corporation, who has generously supported the receptions held to honor this project.

I want to thank those who have been an invaluable help to both the Museum and Joshua as this project unfolded. Jenny Bagert and Edward Hebert, who assist Pailet at his A Gallery for Fine Photography in New Orleans and are artists in their own right, have been active in keeping the Museum connected to the Gallery and assisting Joshua in printing and cataloguing the photographs in this exhibition. I also want to acknowledge his printer, David Zietz in Baton Rouge, who has done a masterful job in producing these prints under Joshua's direction for this exhibition. In addition, I would like to thank the collectors who lent works to this exhibition: Robert and Joy Williams, Robert and Malena Puterbaugh, Travis Puterbaugh, and Lindsay Raley and Michelle Chandler-Raley

The Museum's curatorial staff has worked diligently on this important project. Without them the walls would be bare. I especially want to acknowledge our Curator of Art, Adam Justice, for his passion for this first major project under his management, for his care in its development and details. It was an exciting curatorial process of selection. We worked together with Joshua first in New Orleans and later at the Museum, while we edited from thousands of photographs to form the cohesive and compelling group of images presented here. All but two of these works are of America. The two that are not are included as examples of Joshua's American eye abroad, showing the strength of his view.

Finally, and most certainly, I would like to thank Joshua Mann Pailet for this opportunity to exhibit his photographs and for being the quintessential artist, defined by professionalism and passion. This has been a rewarding and collaborative effort undertaken as a journey of discovery. "Eye See America" unfolded and is presented as a visual essay where "every picture tells a story." Each is worthy of the time it takes to decode their meanings and messages. Please enjoy these marvelous views as captured by Joshua Mann Pailet on his travels around America.

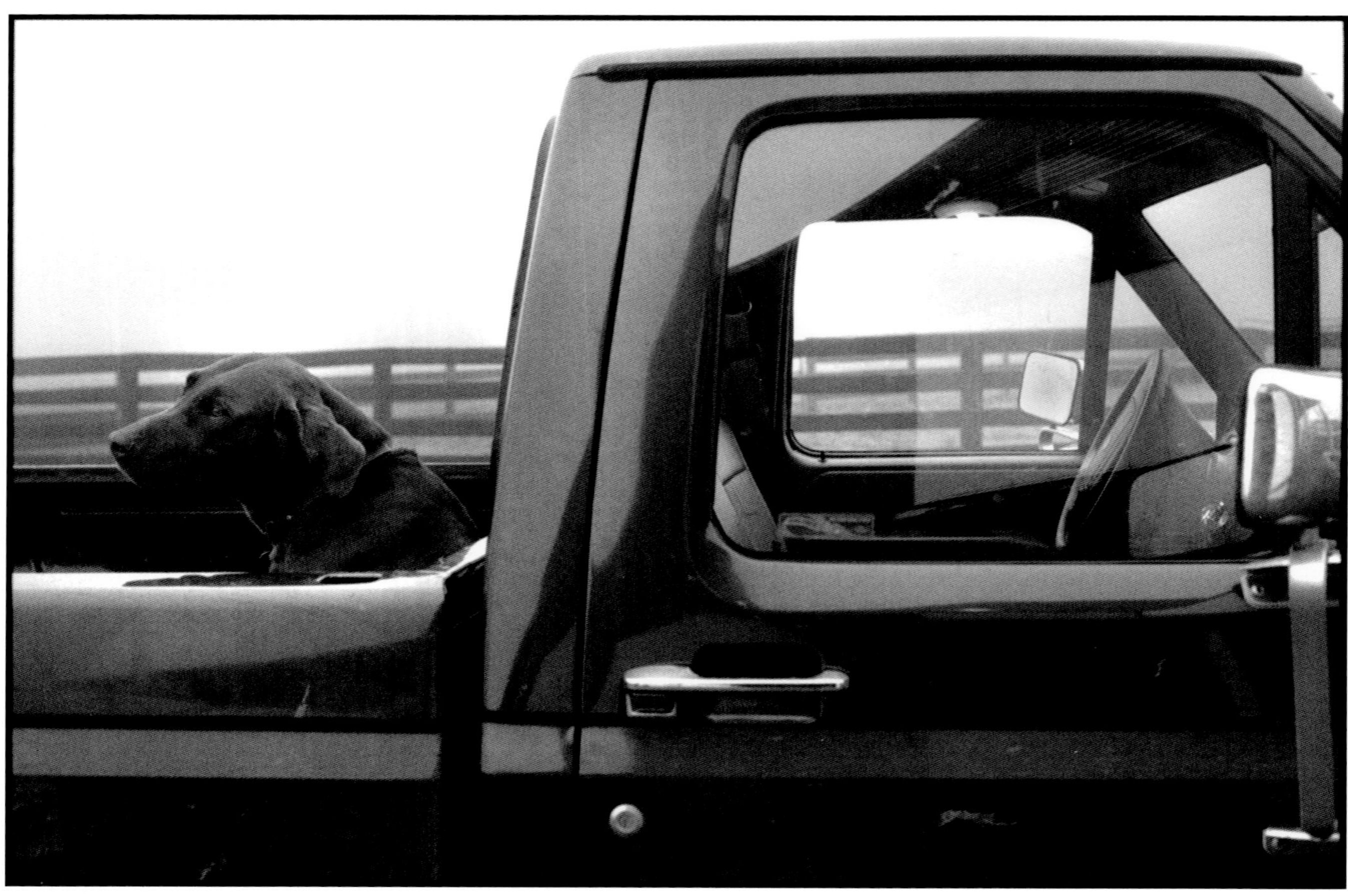

Sam's Dog, Boudin, 1993
Virginia

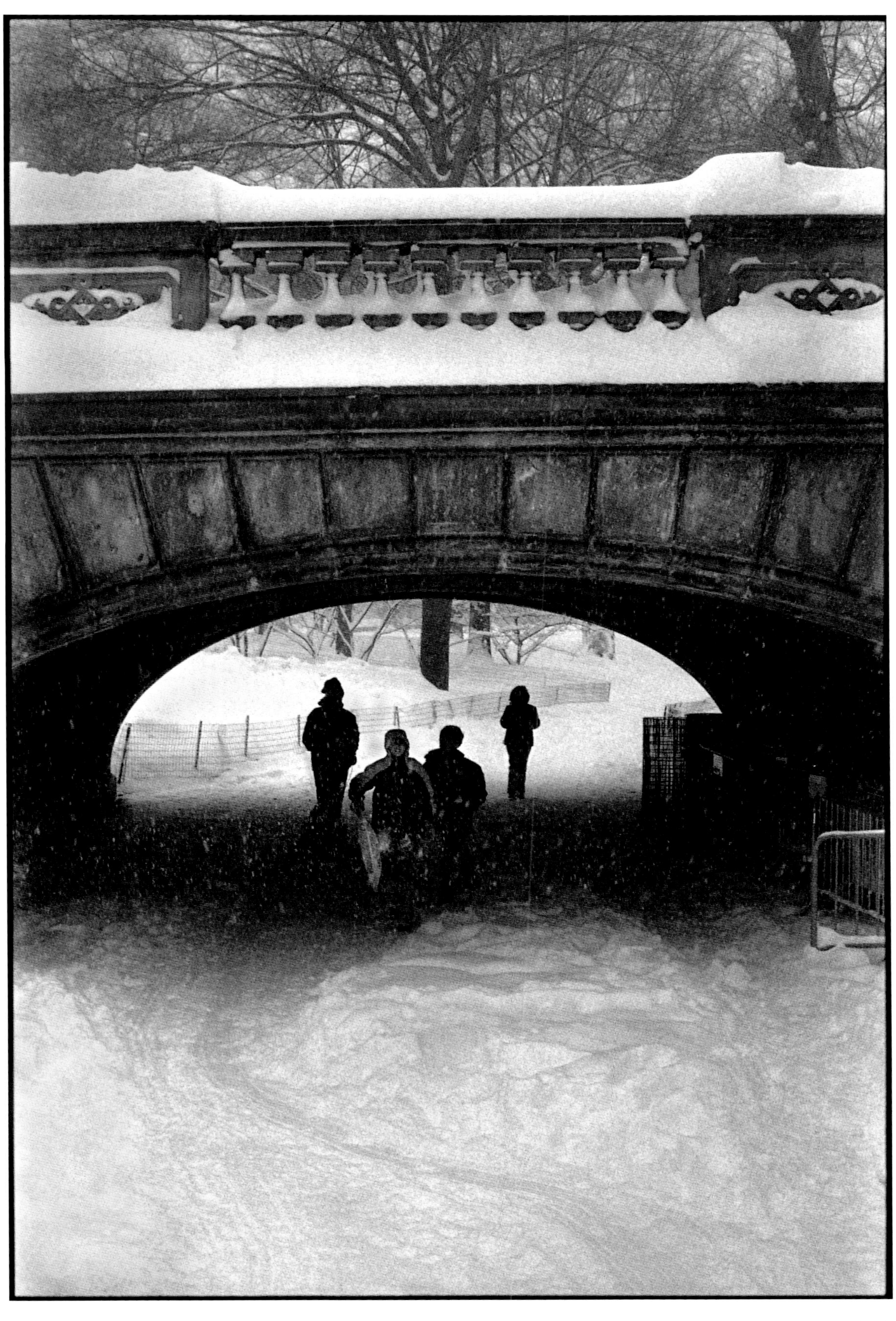

The Blizzard, 2006
New York, NY

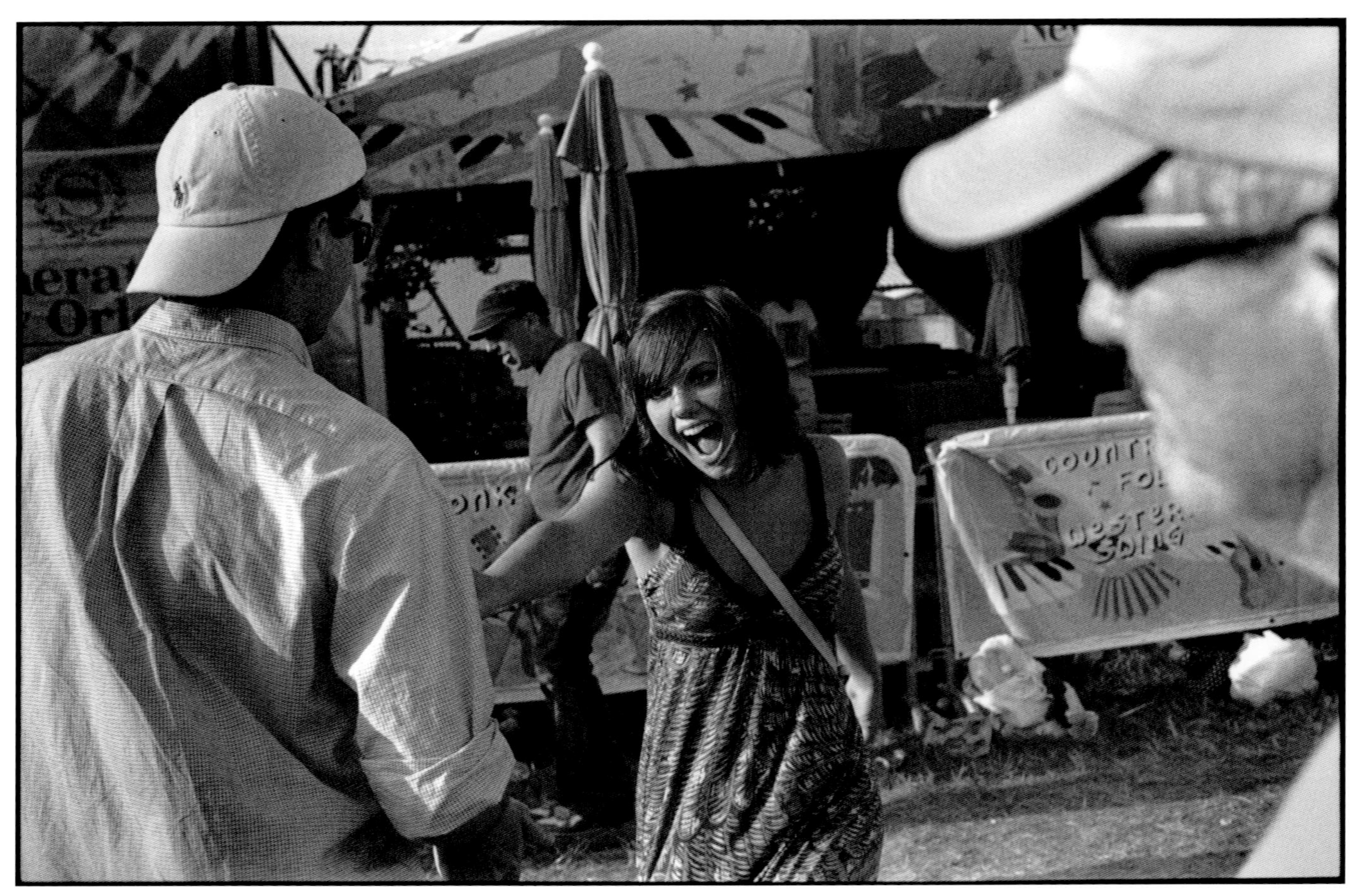

She Dances, 2009
New Orleans, LA

INTRODUCTION

by Robert E. Puterbaugh

This exhibit is the natural progression of other great photography exhibits at Polk Museum of Art which are directly related, in various ways, to Joshua Mann Pailet. The history of photography includes giants such as Henri Cartier-Bresson, Ansel Adams. Jerry Uelsmann, Herman Leonard, Yousuf Karsh, and Elliott Erwitt. All of these photographers have been exhibited in the past several years at Polk Museum of Art. All have also been represented by Joshua at his gallery in New Orleans. Most importantly, all have, through their friendship with Joshua, influenced him in his progression to become one of the leading photographers of modern American life. It is only fitting that this current exhibit, *Eye See America: Through the Lens of Joshua Mann Pailet*, continues the series of great photography exhibits at Polk Museum of Art.

My own relationship with Joshua began many years ago in the French Quarter of New Orleans, when I first entered Joshua's *A Gallery for Fine Photography* and he introduced me to the photography of Yousuf Karsh. This introduction would lead to close friendships with Joshua and other noted photographers, including the greatest Jazz photographer in history, Herman Leonard. Since that time, Joshua and I have traveled many roads together, have experienced the tragedy of Hurricane Katrina, and have worked together, both at Polk Museum of Art and at his gallery in New Orleans, organizing exhibits featuring the works of Yousuf Karsh, Herman Leonard, Jenny Bagert and most recently, Jessica Lange.

The importance of Joshua Mann Pailet in the world of photography is vast and varied. His gallery on Chartres Street in New Orleans is recognized as one of, if not the finest, photography galleries in the world. Joshua has taught photography and has designed and produced many books on photography, including *Linda McCartney Photographs: Sun Prints and Platinums*. His own photography has been the subject of the books *All Aboard America, the American Freedom Train* and *The World's Fair, New Orleans*. His photographs are included in many important museums and private collections. His delightfully comedic photograph, *Man and Apes*, is in the permanent collection of Polk Museum of Art and is included in this exhibition.

Joshua is such a prolific artist, and the body of his work is so vast, that the most difficult part of curating this current exhibit has been deciding which photographs to include. Dan Stetson, Adam Justice and I have spent many hours, both in Lakeland and in New Orleans, viewing thousands of Joshua's beautiful photographs, all of which are worthy of being included in this exhibit. In making the final curatorial selection, Dan and Adam have done a marvelous job of selecting a broad cross section of Joshua's work which hopefully will allow the viewer to appreciate the artistic vision of Joshua Mann Pailet.

When I have viewed Joshua's photographs over the years, *Eye See* photographs which express Joshua's unique ability to capture the essence of America and its people. I have traveled this country through Joshua's eyes, whether those eyes have put me on board *The American Freedom Train* or allowed me to celebrate the *World's Fair* or walk through the city of New Orleans during the aftermath of Hurricane Katrina. Wherever I have traveled through Joshua's Eyes, I have been able to experience a unique view of this country and its people and in many cases, visit a moment passed which will never return. I am so pleased that others, who view the photographs in this catalog or on the walls of Polk Museum of Art during this exhibit, will now also be able to *See America Through the Lens of Joshua Mann Pailet*.

A SENSITIVE LENS ON AMERICA

by Adam Justice, Curator of Art

American flags line a mid-western street running past a police officer outside a loan office; a sign which reads "all conversions approximate" hangs above an auctioneer who acknowledges bids on a painted portrait of Christ as an African American attendant lingers in the background; a man's profile is silhouetted before an infinite sea of people at an arena rock concert; an elegant lady escapes the crowd at a Washington DC art gallery for a cigarette; and an elderly woman slouches hopelessly in a hotel's luggage cart on a street ravaged by Hurricane Katrina. Such images are powerful testimonies to the oscillating appearance of America's social landscape. When combined, they form a comprehensive forty year panoramic view of America through the lens of a New Orleans photographer. Joshua Mann Pailet wields his camera much like an autobiographer pushes a pen, using a first-person perspective to record fractals of the American condition. Yet, Pailet utilizes the integrity of the photographed image to illustrate more than his own experience; he also illustrates the broader phenomena of American society, thus linking to our shared national psyche.

Documentary photography is such a literal art; the unadulterated image provides room for interpretation, but prohibits you from questioning what is before you. This is the rawest form of fine art photography, unaffected by digital manipulation, recognizable and representational. The unrefined realism of such photographs can sometimes pose questions or create commentaries that other more subjective art forms (such as painting) cannot. This fits comfortably within the general American context and affection for the physical, the here and the now. It makes sense, therefore, that documentary photography, initiated through photojournalism, has become such a formidable means of recording the progression of modern American culture. The implication being that contemporary photographers are the informed witnesses to our temporal and physical environments.

The history of documentary photography traces back to 1900 when George Eastman, founder of the Eastman Kodak Company in Rochester, NY, introduced the Brownie camera. This inexpensive hand-held camera was the first of its kind and made photography accessible to the American masses, allowing it to gain broad acceptance among the various social classes. American

artists and amateurs alike became fascinated by the new imaging process and its ability to capture such an acute sense of realism. This catapulted the popularity of photojournalism and bolstered the reputation of photography as a serious means of pictorial representation in America. Scenes of daily American life became a popular subject as everyone turned their cameras toward what they knew best: their family, their hometowns and the events that shaped their lives.

Artists expanded photography into an art form by documenting their surroundings with special attention paid to those formal elements traditionally reserved for painting, most notably composition, lighting, perspective and content. This was especially true for early American photographers who were inspired by the multifaceted nature of American culture. Their photographs began to be the primary means for conveying a sense of American society to the rest of the world. Additionally, Americans began to regard photographs as a reflection of themselves and the national identity of which they were a part. Emerging fine art photographers gave equal attention to the hardships and accomplishments of American life. Dorothea Lange influenced documentary photography through her images of the devastating result of the Great Depression of the early 1930s. Photographer and environmentalist Ansel Adams popularized the raw beauty of the American west through his photographs. Diane Arbus exposed a lesser known side of American life through her photographs of subjects with eccentric personalities and physical deformities. Aaron Siskind extracts paint, cement and metal forms from their recognizable urban environments to produce flat abstract photographs related to Abstract Expressionist paintings. Cindy Sherman renews the self-portrait, photographing herself in fictional scenes similar to Hollywood stills thereby referencing how Americans often attempt to imitate the famous and the fictional.

Contemporary American photographers continue recording the content behind a national identity by capturing aspects of the current state of the union. They are, of course, inspired and influenced by different stimuli than their predecessors, but it is intriguing to realize how they all share similar intent. As frames of mind shift and force our attention to other, newer characteristics of the American socialscape, photographers record the progressing content of our American lives. Ongoing developments in technology, politics, finance, popular culture and religion make up the fodder upon which our senses constantly feed and then abandon with little time to fully process. Through their images, contemporary photographers help us retain what our senses have been conditioned to continuously replace with more current information. These photographs become the immediate visual history of the present tense, prolonging and preserving semblances of what we have already failed to remember.

Joshua Mann Pailet is a distinctive American photographer. This statement is not intended to affirm the obvious, but to underscore the evident. His ability to capture what we fail to recognize is due to his photographer's eye, partly a result of him being so completely immersed in his present experience, keeping his camera hanging from one shoulder, ready to aim a focused lens in any direction. This is certainly a valuable characteristic for any photographer amid the modern slick pace of American society; the current visual era we have all grown into seldom allows for delayed reactions. However, it is not only Pailet's quick reaction to what stimuli may come and go that makes his photographs so powerful. He has the conditioned eye of a photographer; moreover, his is the sharp eye of an artist, always sensitive to composition and light. It is important to clarify that Pailet perfectly addresses all of the interrogatives of contemporary documentary photography: where, when, who, and how. It is easy to recognize that his creative synapses never cease and that we are certainly the privileged beneficiaries of the results.

In all respects, Pailet's photographs succeed where words are void of adequate impact. Their visual appeal dismisses the importance of conversation, validating that to see is to feel and to feel is to know. As with earlier American photographers, Pailet's crisp black-and-white images derive from one unique perspective, but are simultaneously relative to an entire population. What makes him so remarkably different, however, is how he never completely separates himself from the exposed image. He is rarely physically present in these images, but instead is represented by these images being so directly tied to his own experiences. Additionally, his photographs are not totally sanctioned by society or personality, but tempered by his ability to make his American experience relate so well with our own. Although we, as spectators, can respond to these photographs in various ways, they are never our views and memories. Part of their appeal is how they collectively form a composite portrait of the artist, gradually

constructed over thousands of rolls of film. This is rare and often unsuccessfully achieved through documentary photography because the process often omits all signs of what art historians refer to as the hand of the artist, or respective style.

Documentary photographers must rely on their respective points of perspective and what they choose to convey through the finished image, which is commonly empirical, to define their presence within the work. This is further influenced by how universally relative the images can be, connecting with an audience on a number of levels including recognizable subject matter and content. This ultimately separates a documentary photographer from his work and allows the general public to, in a sense, own the image. Painters are less susceptible to this separation because their styles always distinguish them visually; despite how many times a painting is reproduced. This is certainly not to imply that all fine art photographs look the same, but to stress how difficult it can be for a photographer to differentiate him/herself from their peers.

Pailet succeeds quite beautifully in discerning himself from any typical definition or perception of documentary photography. This exhibition is comprised of images from specific portfolios of Pailet's work and other more general photographs taken selectively but spontaneously. Exhibited together they form a unified view of his experience within contemporary American society. From his cross-country ride aboard the Bicentennial American Freedom Train in 1976, and amid crowds to witness the spectacle of American rock 'n roll, to surviving Hurricane Katrina and the tragic aftermath occurring in his hometown of New Orleans, Pailet presents intimate portraits of modern America which are constructive, revealing and phenomenal. Through his lens, we see characteristics of humanism and place in American culture which do not specifically belong to our own personal experiences, but appeal to our collective American conscious.

In 1976, Pailet accepted the invitation to ride aboard the American Freedom Train and document small town America as it celebrated the nation's bicentennial. This 26-car train visited all 48 of the continental United States and carried artifacts of American history from George Washington's copy of the Constitution to a rock taken from the moon. The photographs taken by Pailet during this period reflect an America of national fervor, reveling in its successes from the previous 200 years: students cheering trackside; small town streets adorned with rows of American flags; and unique views of national monuments. This portfolio reflects the sense of Americana which has come to define a traditional national sentiment. The beauty of these images lies in how Pailet conveys such positivism and patriotism through the faces and places of small town America, which is often overshadowed by the more economically driven face of America. Similar to Lange before him, Pailet turns his lens toward a lesser known facet of American culture, but unlike Lange, his photographs have an overall celebratory and nostalgic appeal.

As a direct contrast to his American Freedom Train portfolio, this exhibition also includes Pailet's emotionally charged photographs of hurricane ravaged New Orleans and how its residents embody the energy to transform tragedy into beauty. These images are powerful testimonies to nature's power, man's vulnerability and humanity's perseverance. Most of these photographs were captured as Pailet steered his bicycle around the flood ridden remains of the city, seeking those images which best defined the leaden atmosphere around him: police officers with rifles wading down city streets; piles of vandalized refuse; and signs of hope as sunlight reveals a receding flood line. From our positions outside of these photographs, having been thus removed from the tragic scene, Pailet offers us a deeper insight into the personal tragedies experienced by those surviving the Hurricane Katrina; these images reflect more realistic accounts than the desensitized flashes and short dialogues from evening news programs. The personal element Pailet implants into these photographs allows us to see what he saw as a survivor of the storm and reveal to us a more affective side of the tragedy.

Joshua Mann Pailet's photographs revolve on an unmistakably American axis pivoted at the intersection of veracity and immediacy. Photographic subtleties and satires are surrendered for a more straightforward commentary on the past and the present states of national identity as seen through the lens of one creative participant. He shares these instances of his own experiences and appeals to our collective unconscious, connecting us through an overarching theme of American culture. These are certainly much more than photographs, they are testaments, they are memorabilia, and they are clear observations into the substance that defines the common core of our modern American existence. Joshua Mann Pailet is first and foremost a fine arts photographer, but additionally he is a biographer of his experiences and, by way of cultural understanding, our own.

CREATIVITY, CONTINUITY, & COLLABORATION

by Joshua Mann Pailet

From the moment in 1971, when the new Nikon camera was in my hand for the first time, I felt and took this picture taking stuff seriously. Every shutter click was to be an important moment worth saving. The photograph is a declaration of my eyewitness experiences.

My Mother, friends, and travels served to inspire. Sharing the blessings I have encountered on this amazing journey is the motive. Seeing the USA and world my reward. Meeting people of all stripes a special gift.

A roll of film per day for nearly forty years, 150,000 black and white negatives and 250,000 Kodachrome slides. People, places, things, and once in a lifetime events. Steam engines, performers, music, festivals, jazz funerals, World's Fair, streets, and characters of New York City, New Orleans, San Francisco, London, Paris, and Prague.

Eye See America salutes my love and passion for Freedom, People, and the USA. It is a vision born of my ancestors and translated with light, time, silver, and paper. It is a tribute to my mother, Charlotte Mann Pailet, my grandparents, Josef and Alma Beran Mann, and my uncle, Jiri Mann.

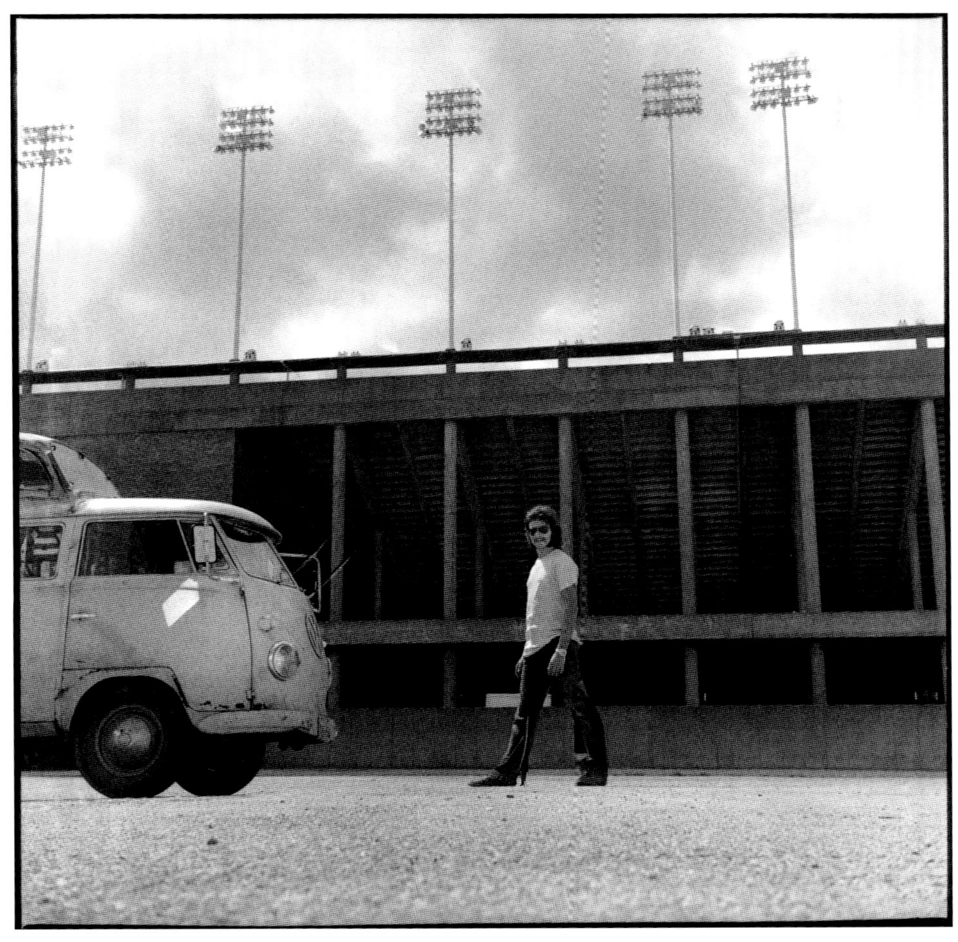

Self-Portrait, 1971
Houston, TX

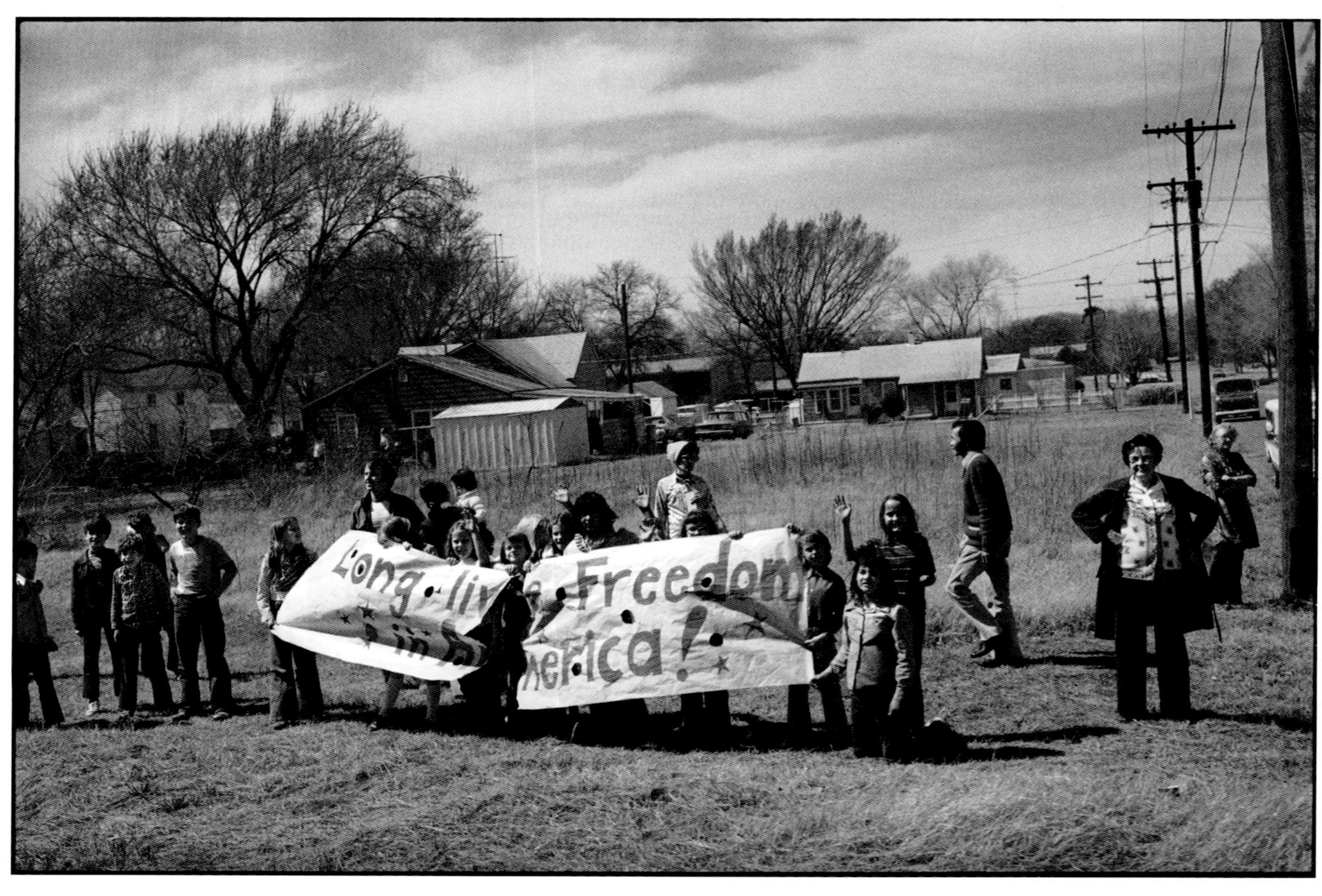

Long Live Freedom, 1976
Kansas

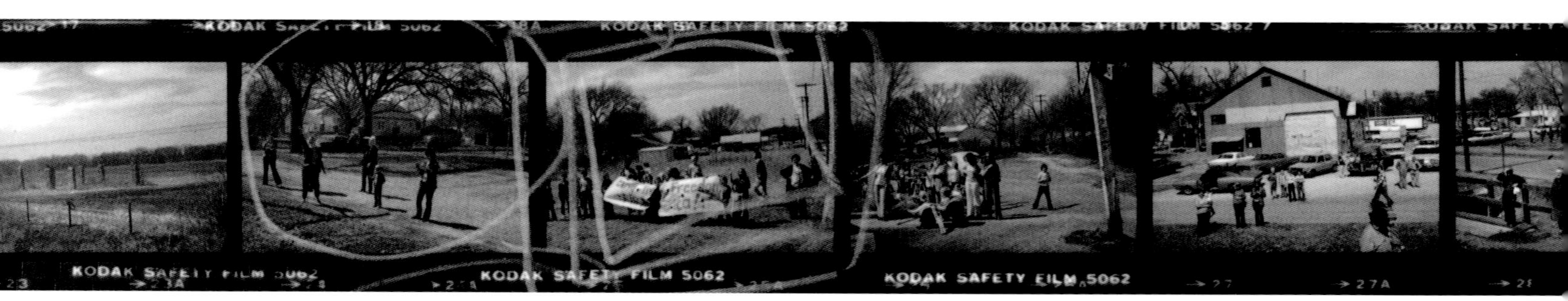

The 4449, American Freedom Train, 1976
Jacksonville, FL

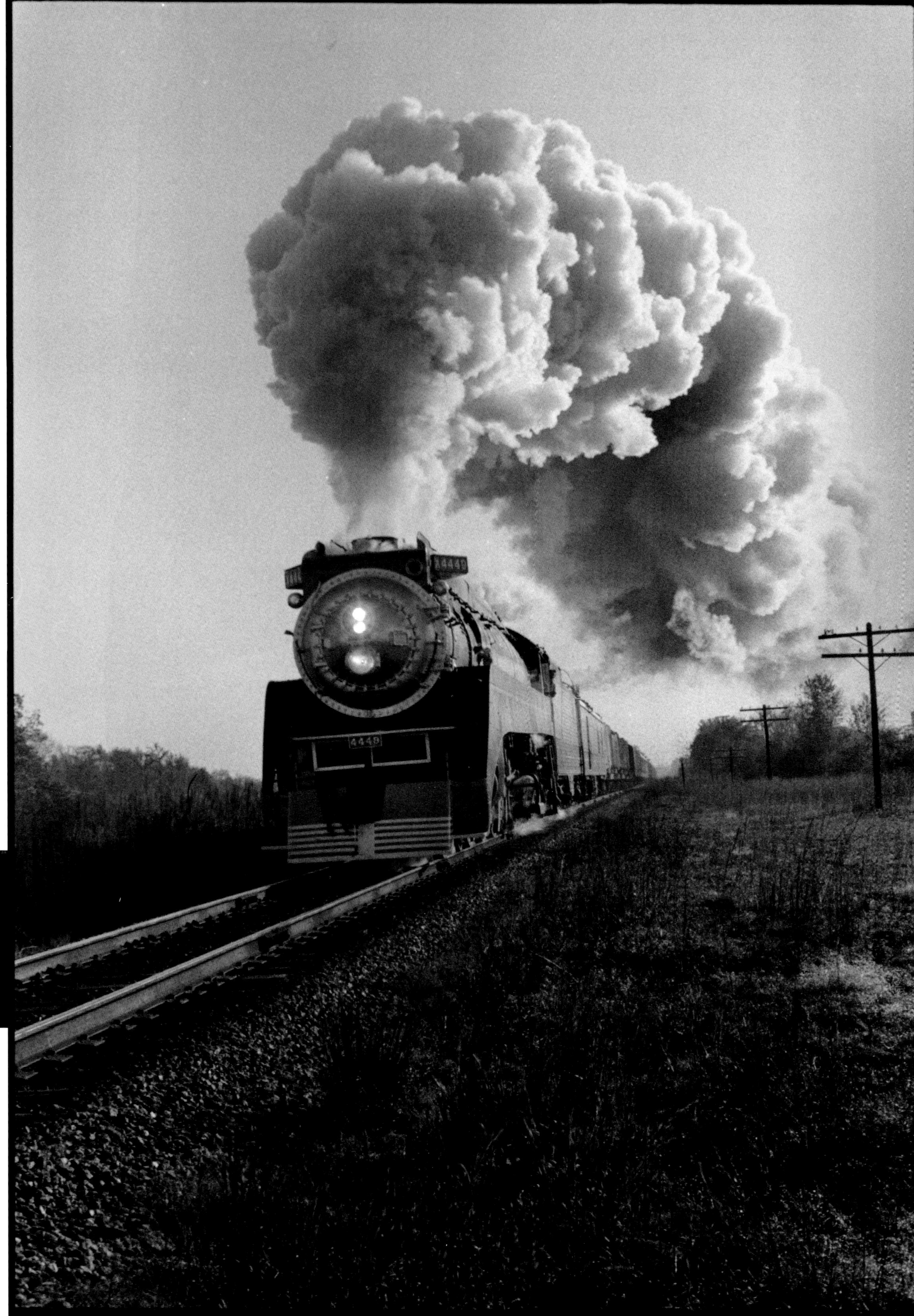
4449
4449

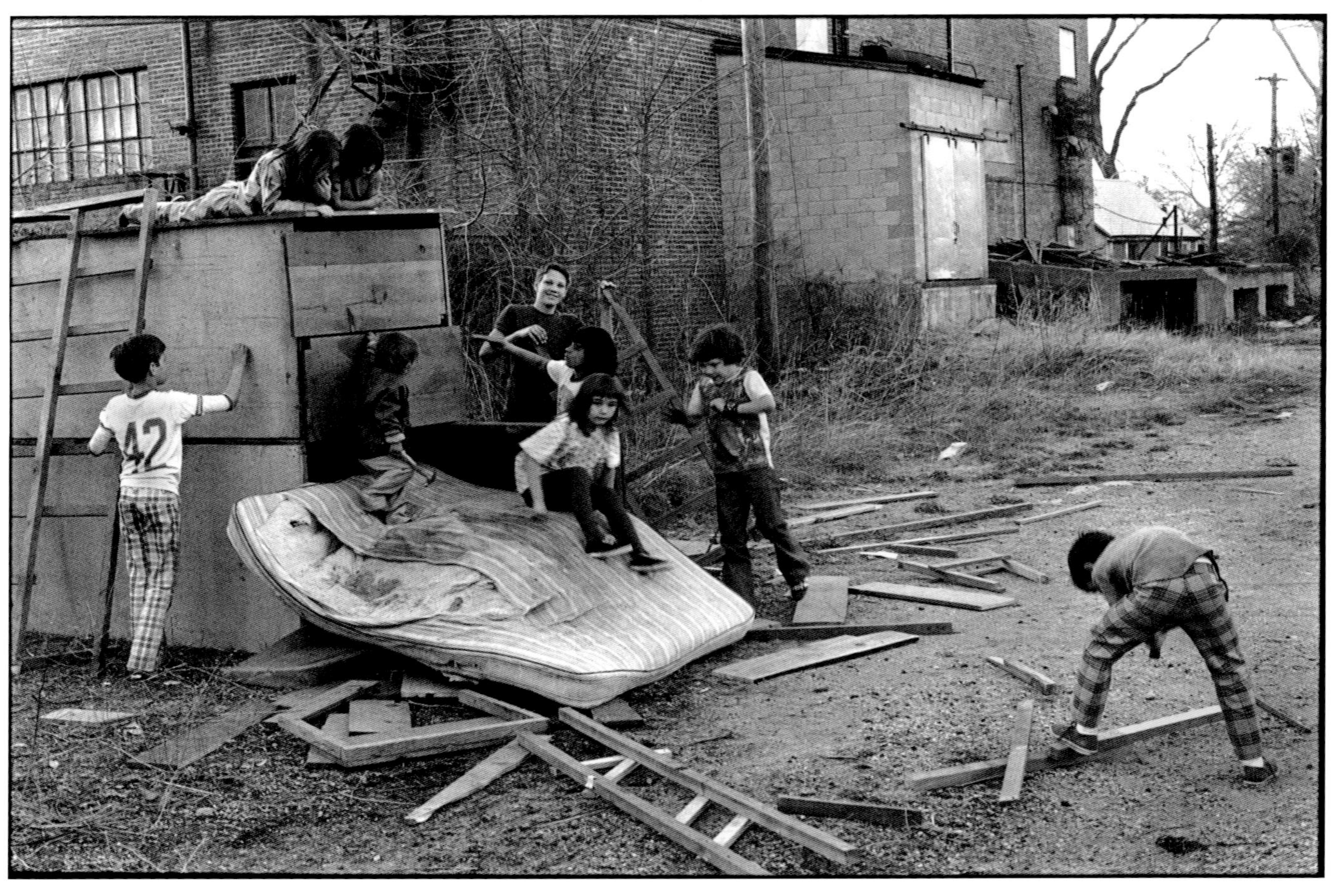

Club House Construction, 1976
Tulsa, OK

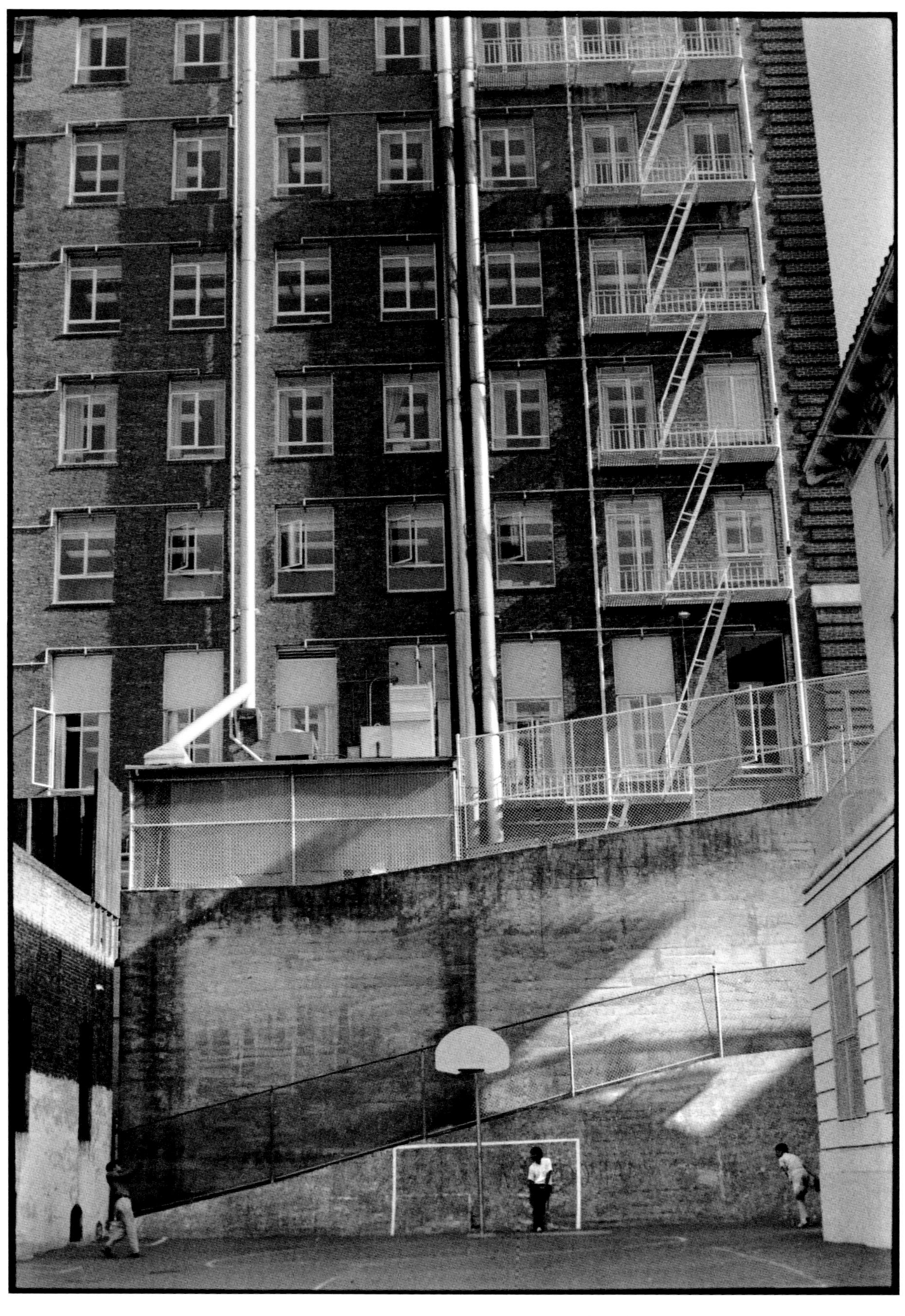

Apartments, Pipes and Sports, 1974
San Francisco, CA

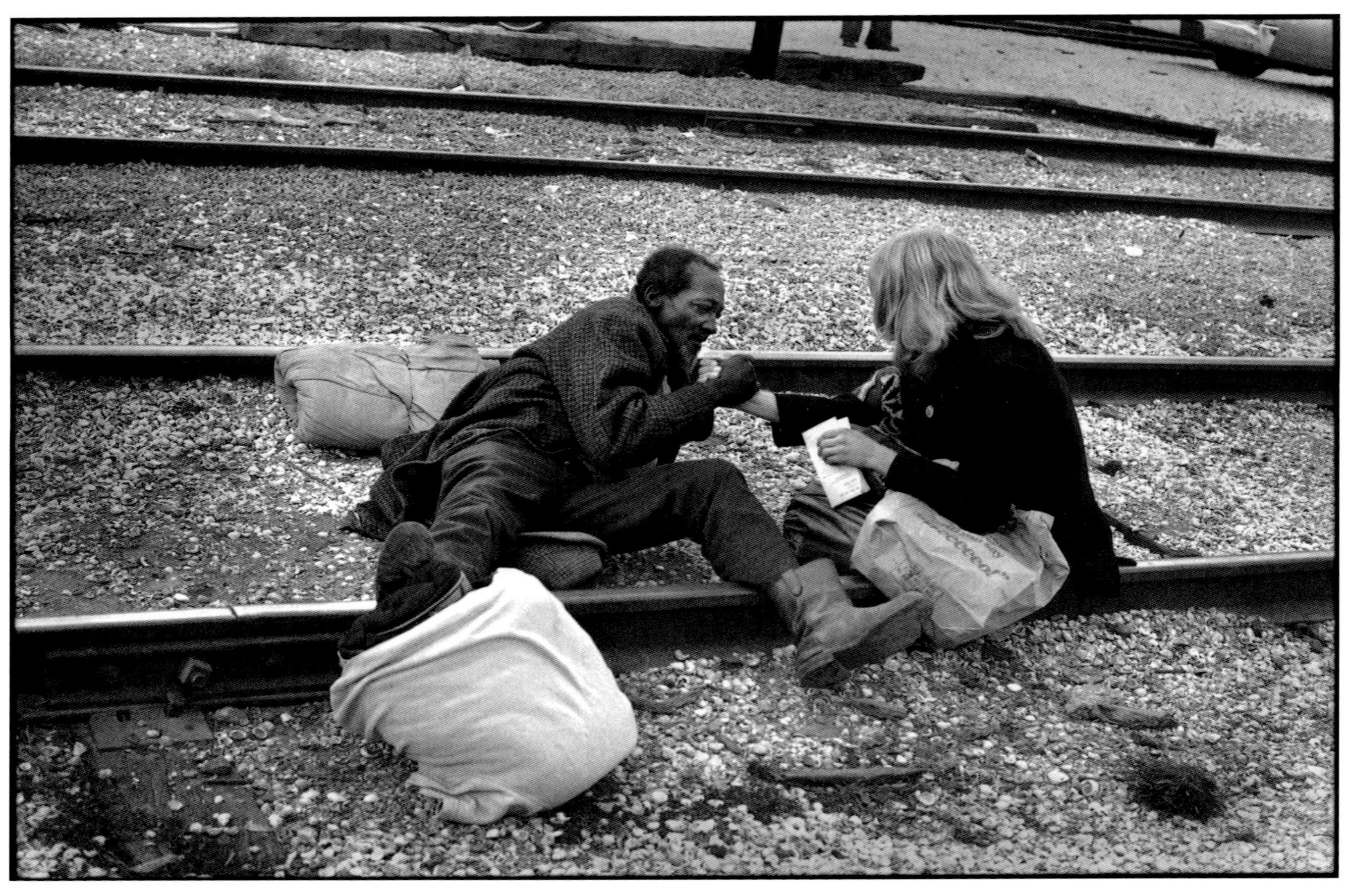

Handshake Tracks, 1974
New Orleans, LA

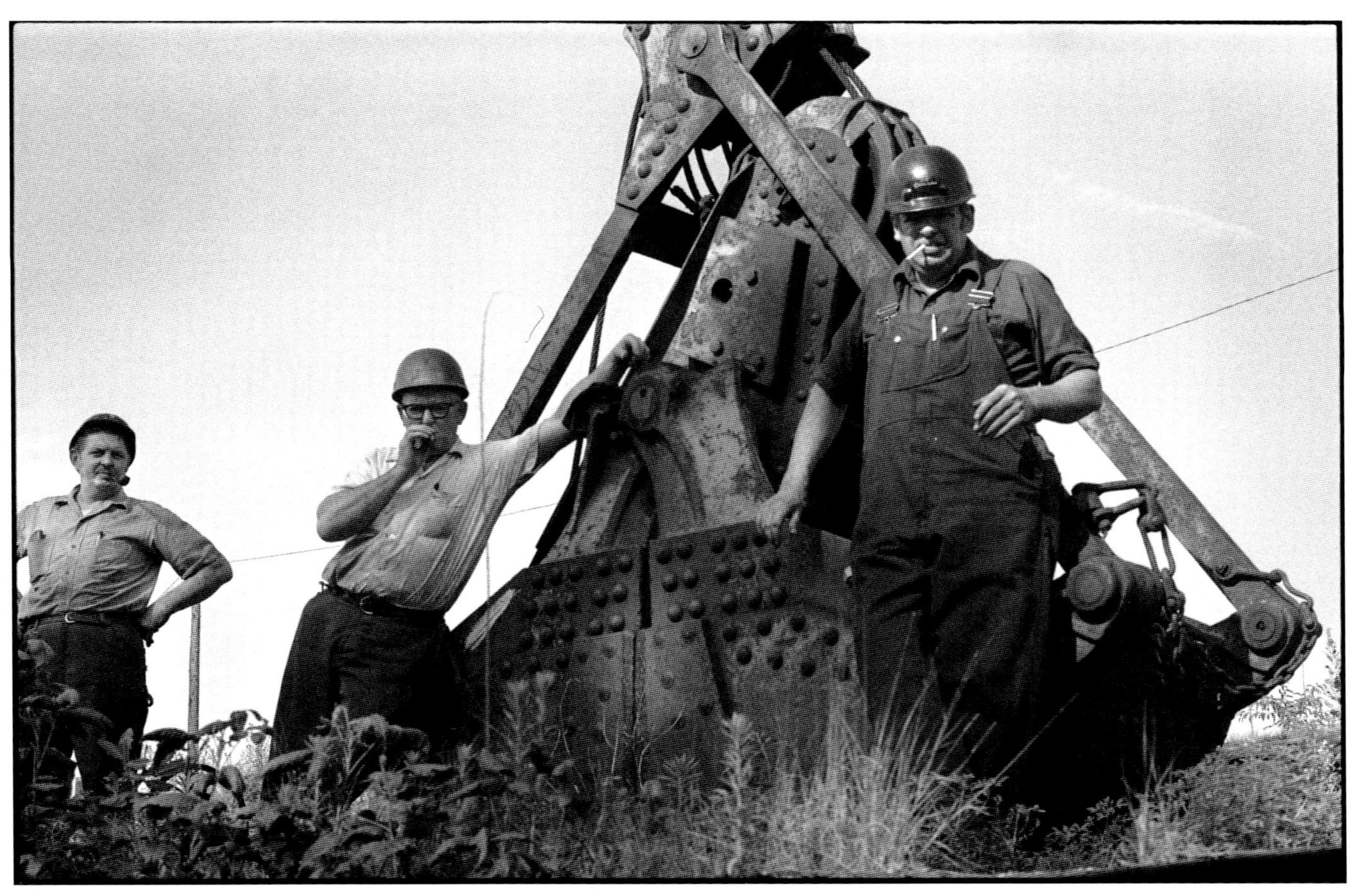

American Workers, 1976
Pennsylvania

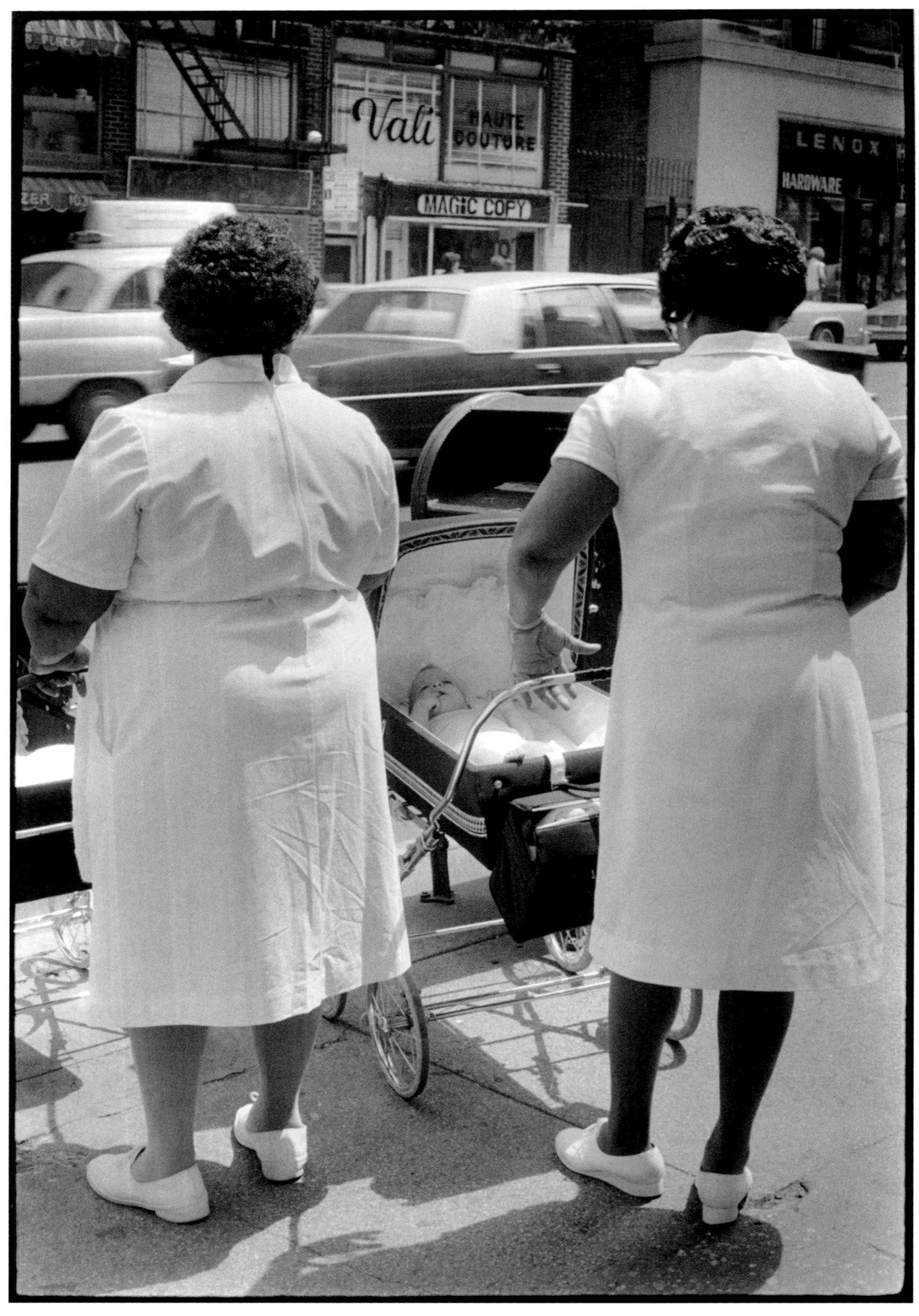

Haute Couture/Magic Copy, 1976
Scranton, PA

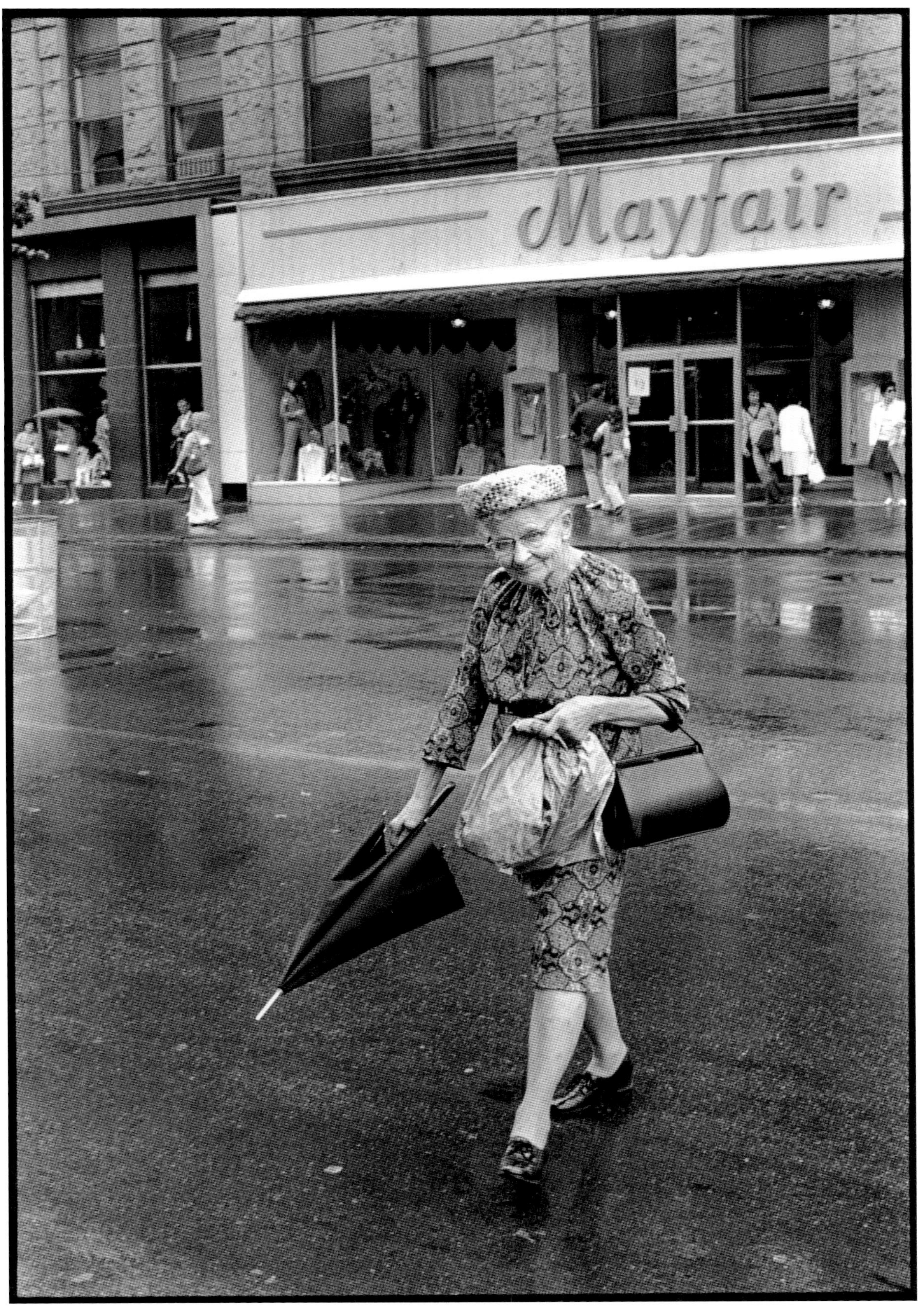

The Mayfair Flirt, 1976
Scranton, PA

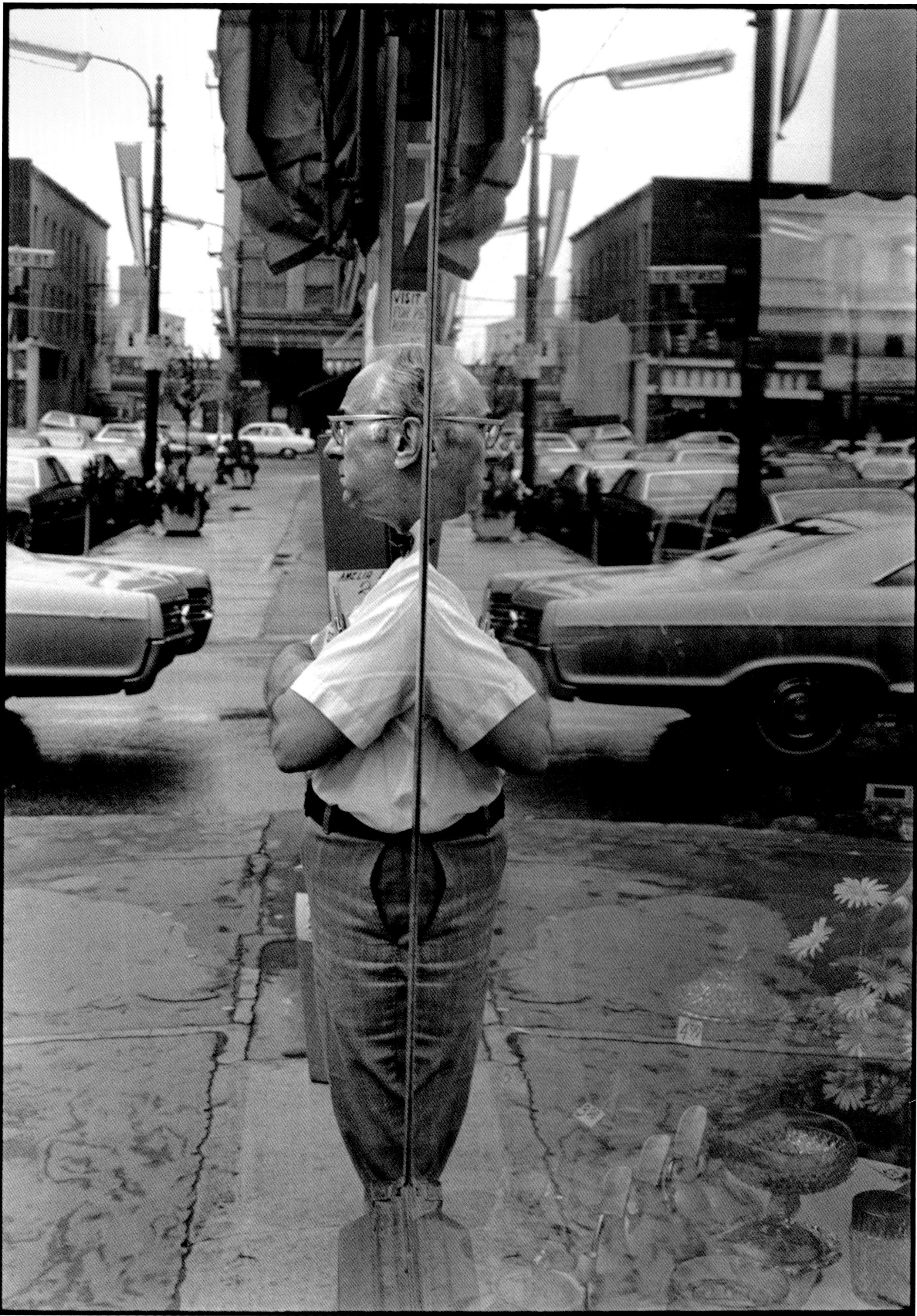

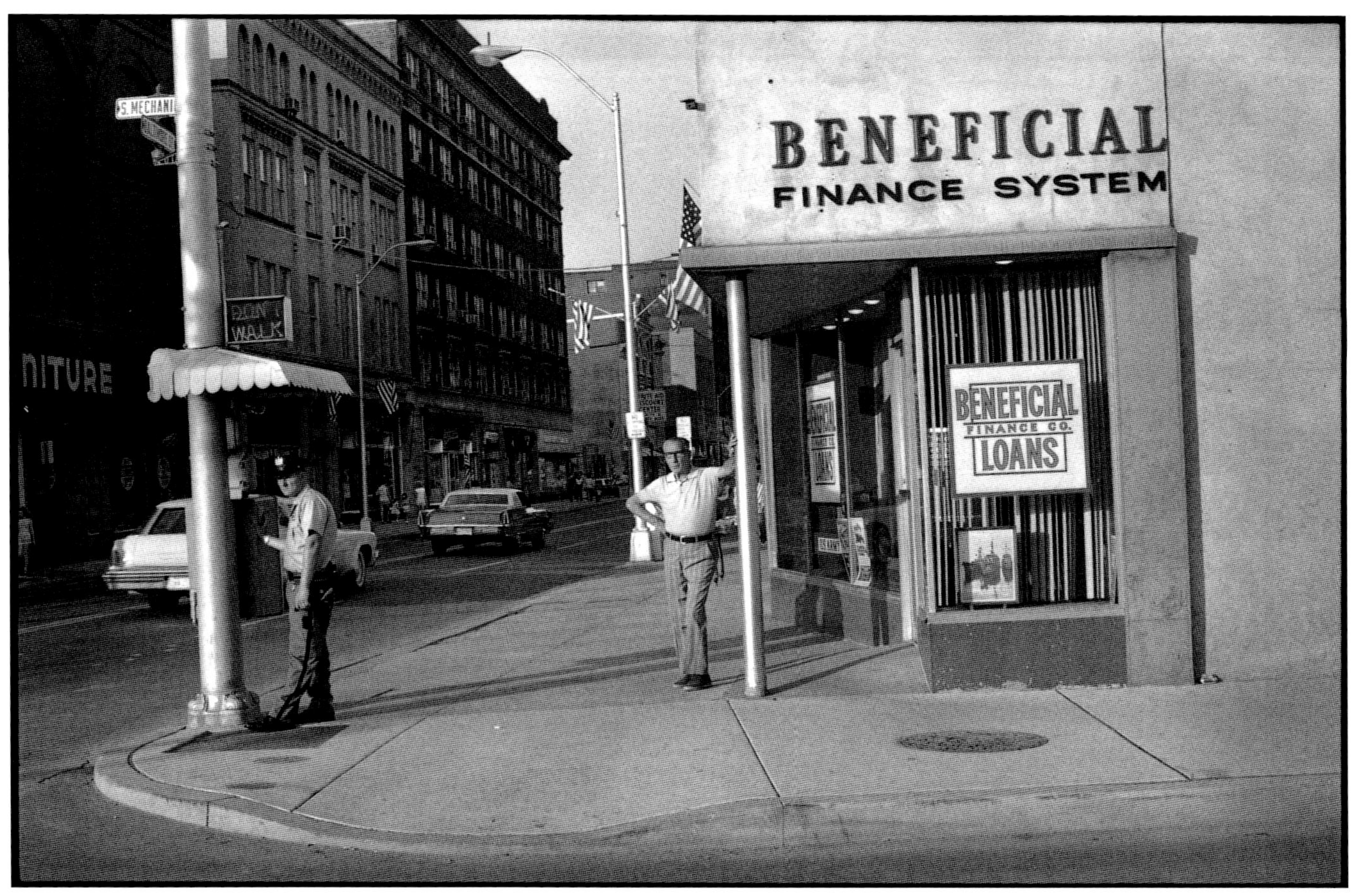

Beneficial Finance System, 1976
Cumberland, MD

Center Street, 1976
Scranton, PA

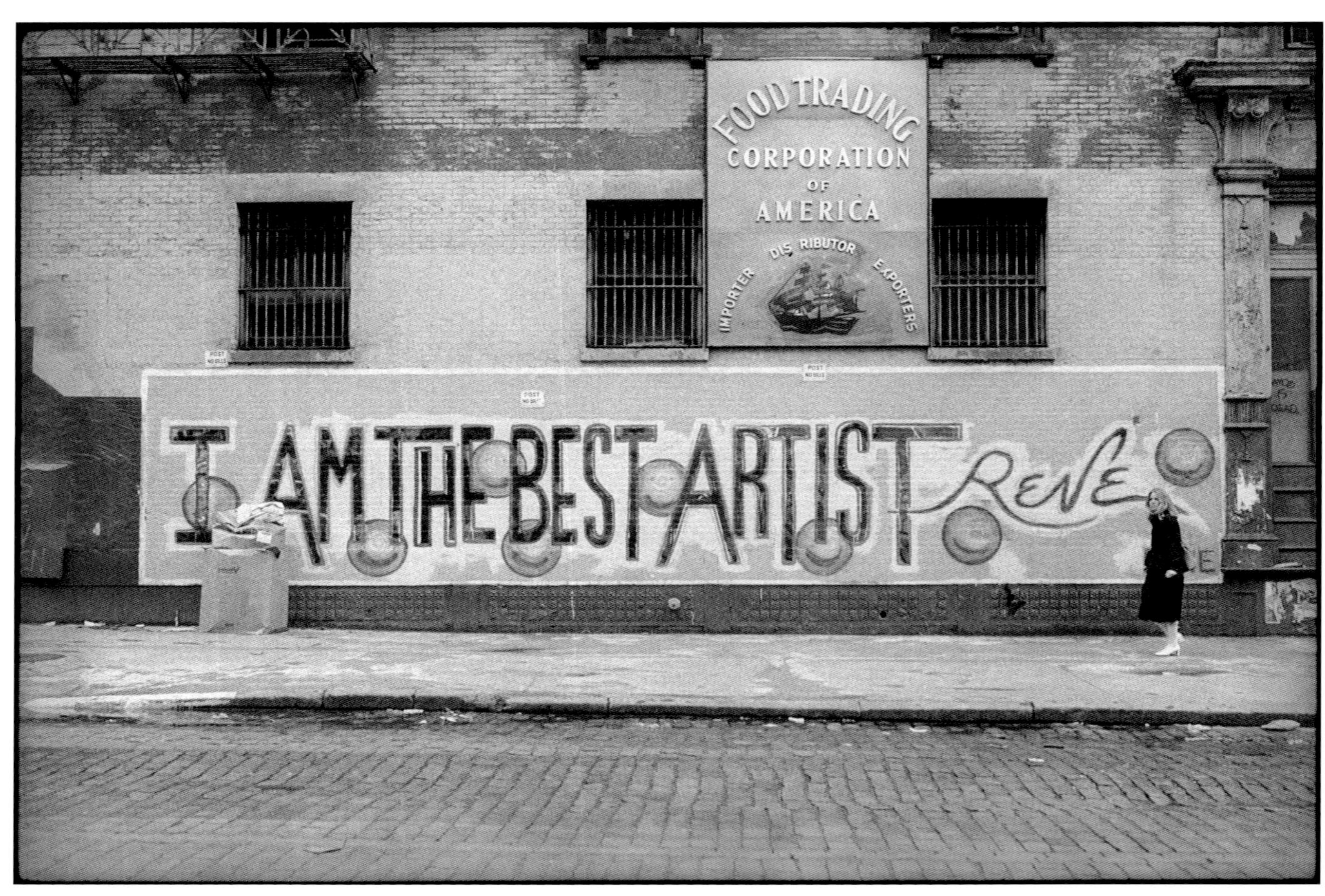

Dream, 1982
New York, NY

Tempo, 1991
New York, NY

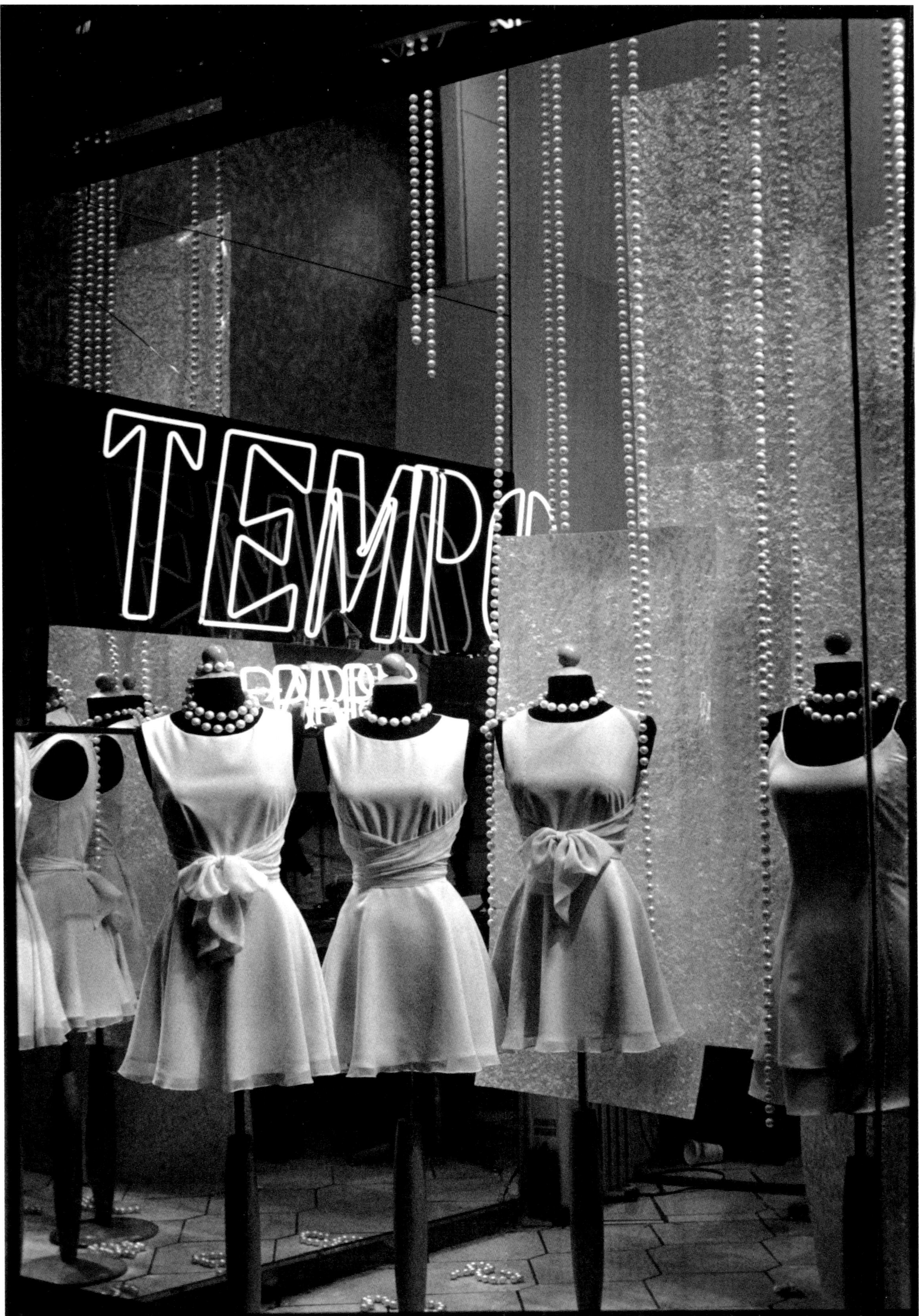

TEMPO

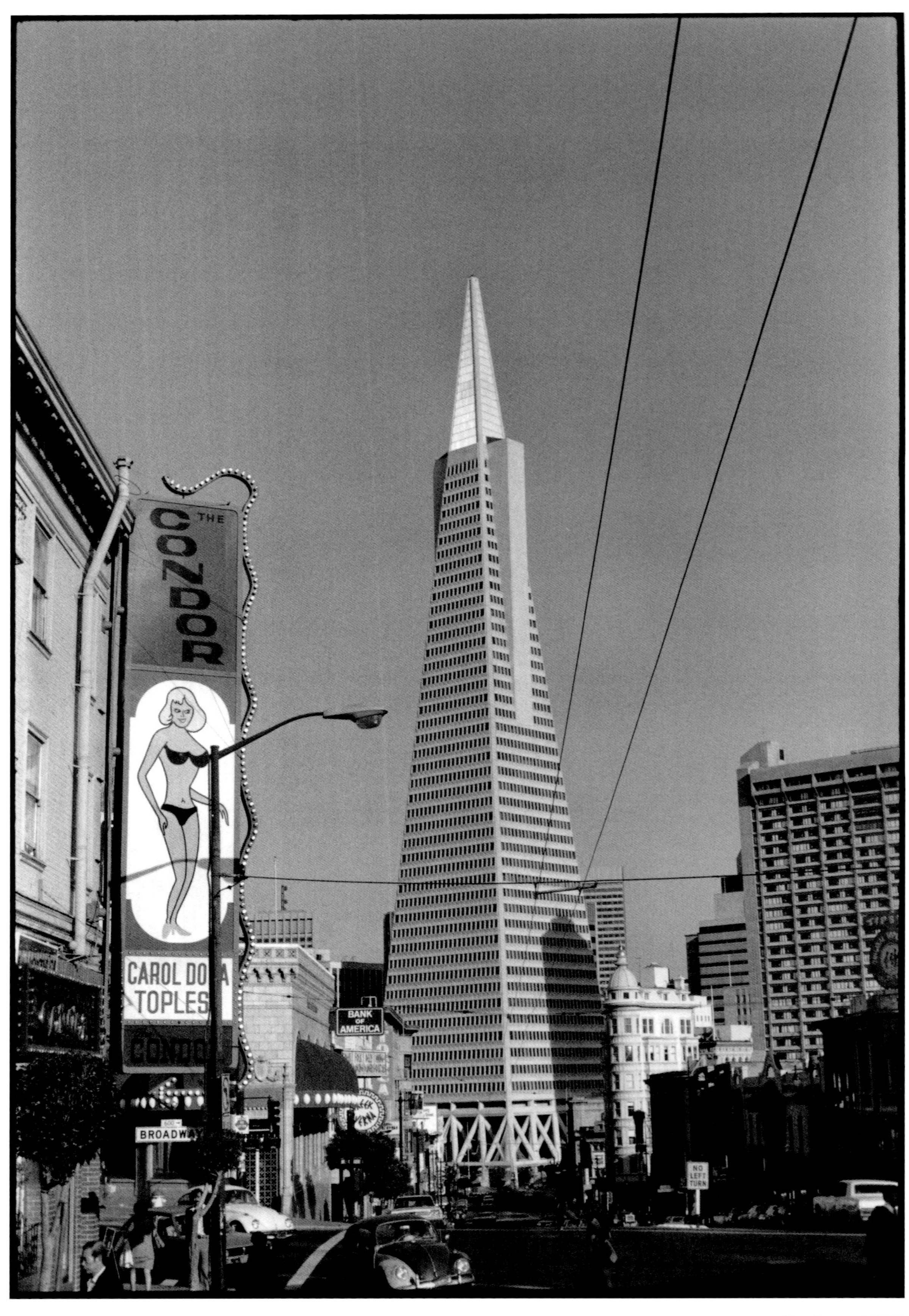

Topless, 1974
San Francisco, CA

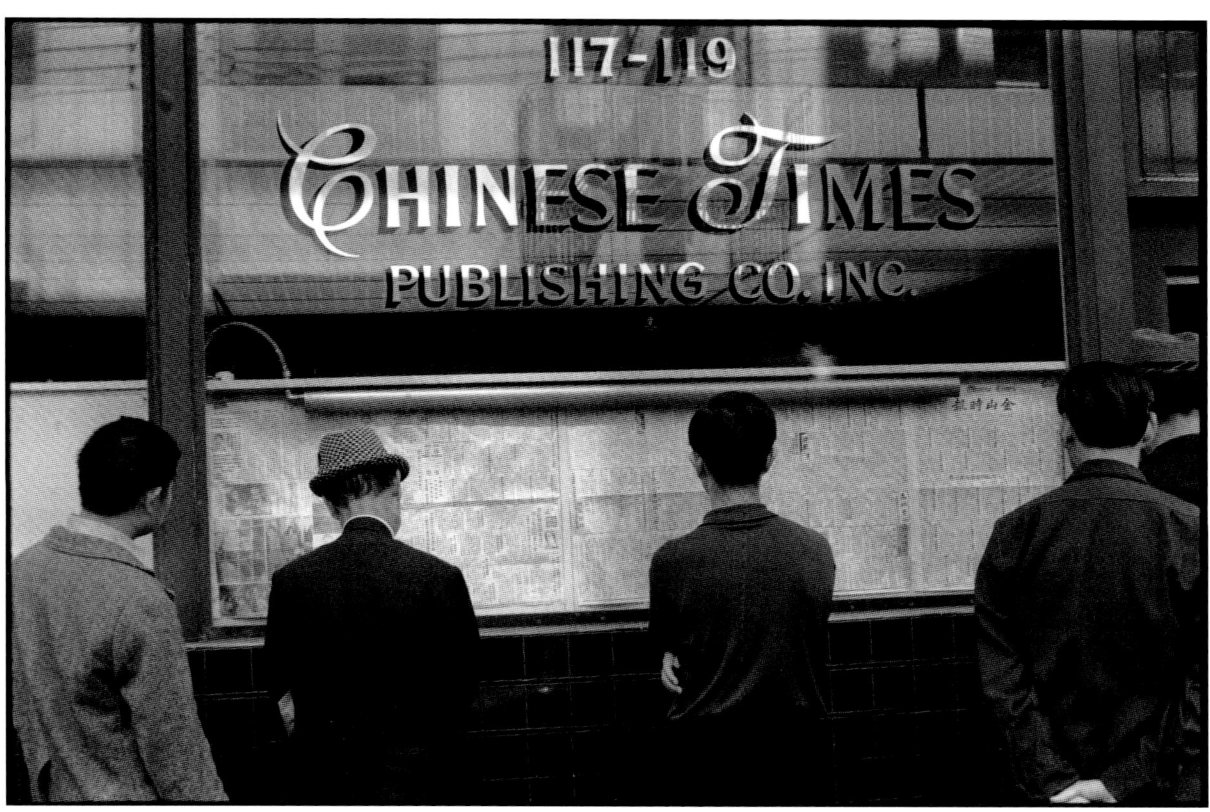

Chinese News, 1974
San Francsco, CA

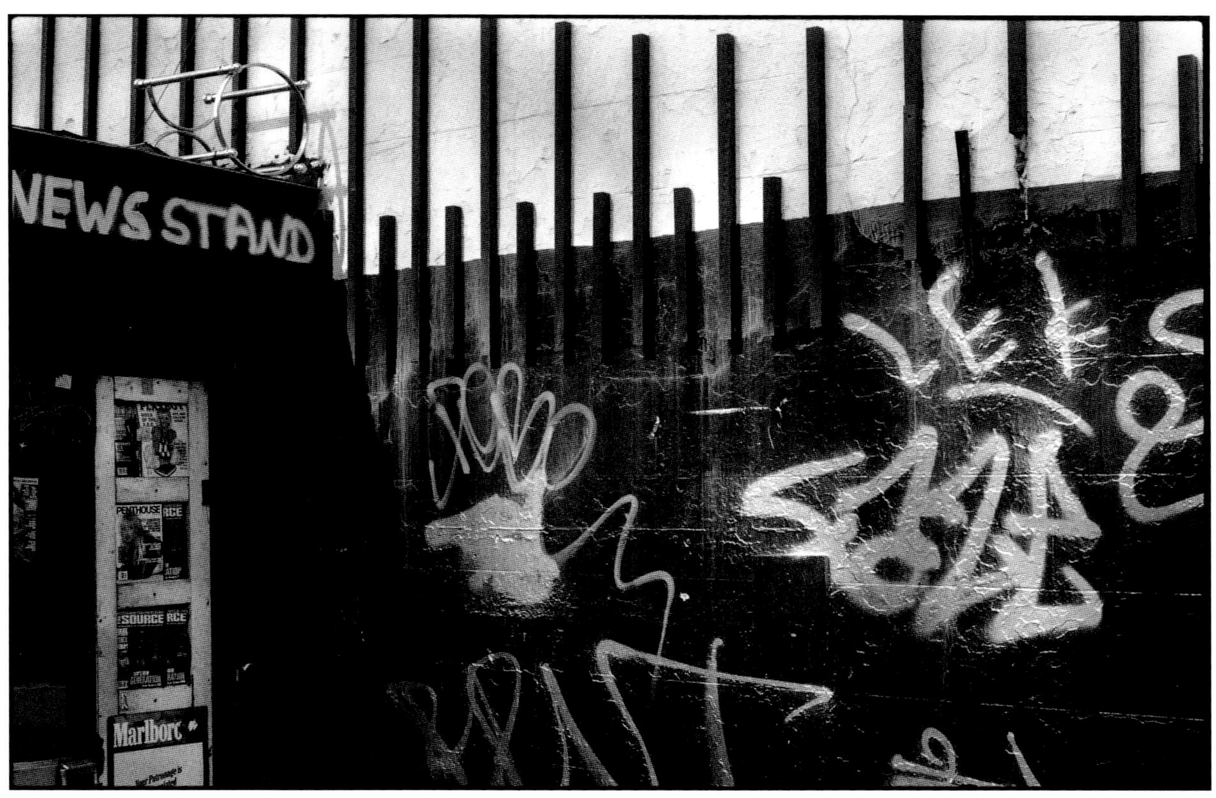

Piano Keys, 1998
New York, NY

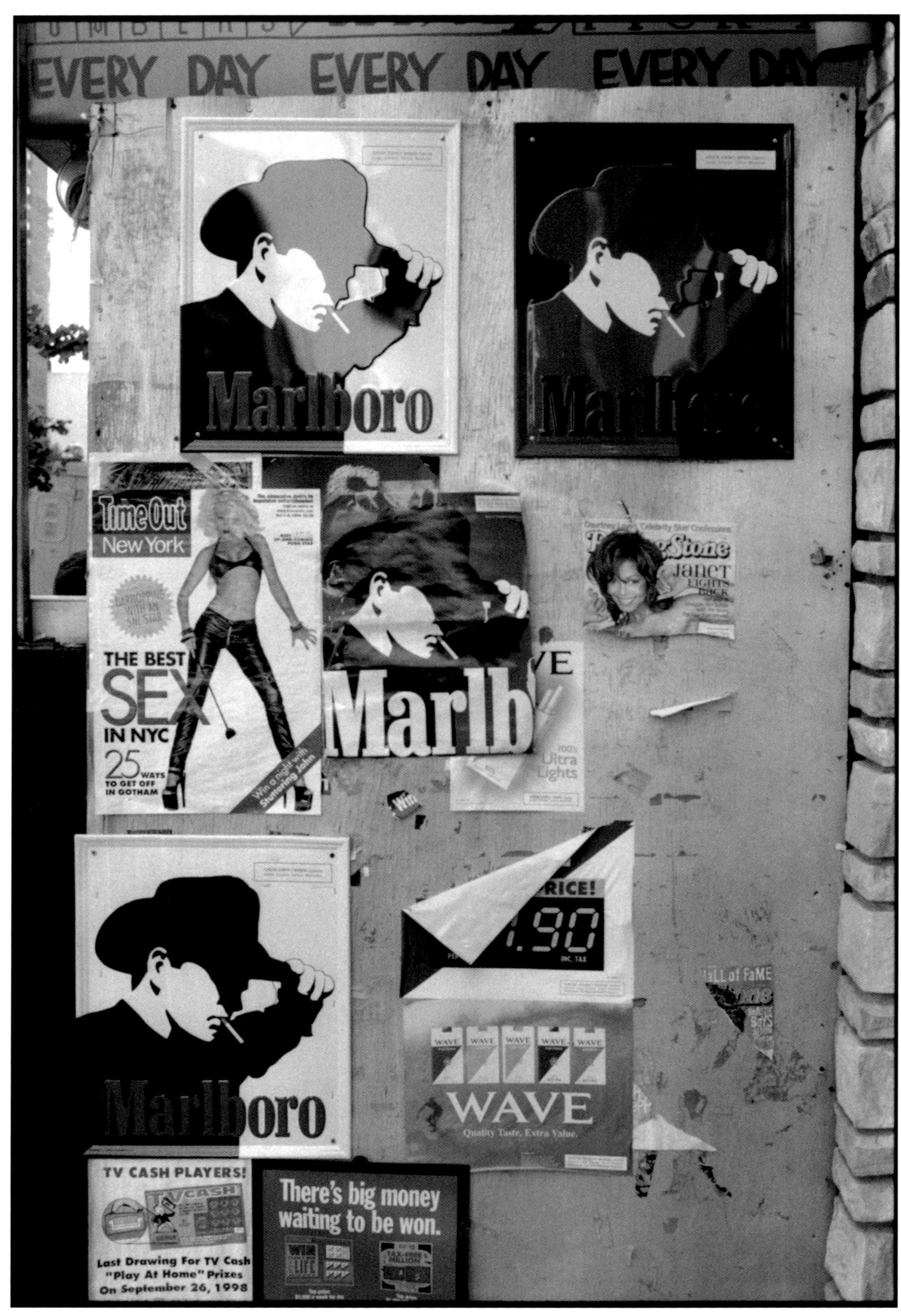

Every Day, Best Sex, Big Money, 1998
New York, NY

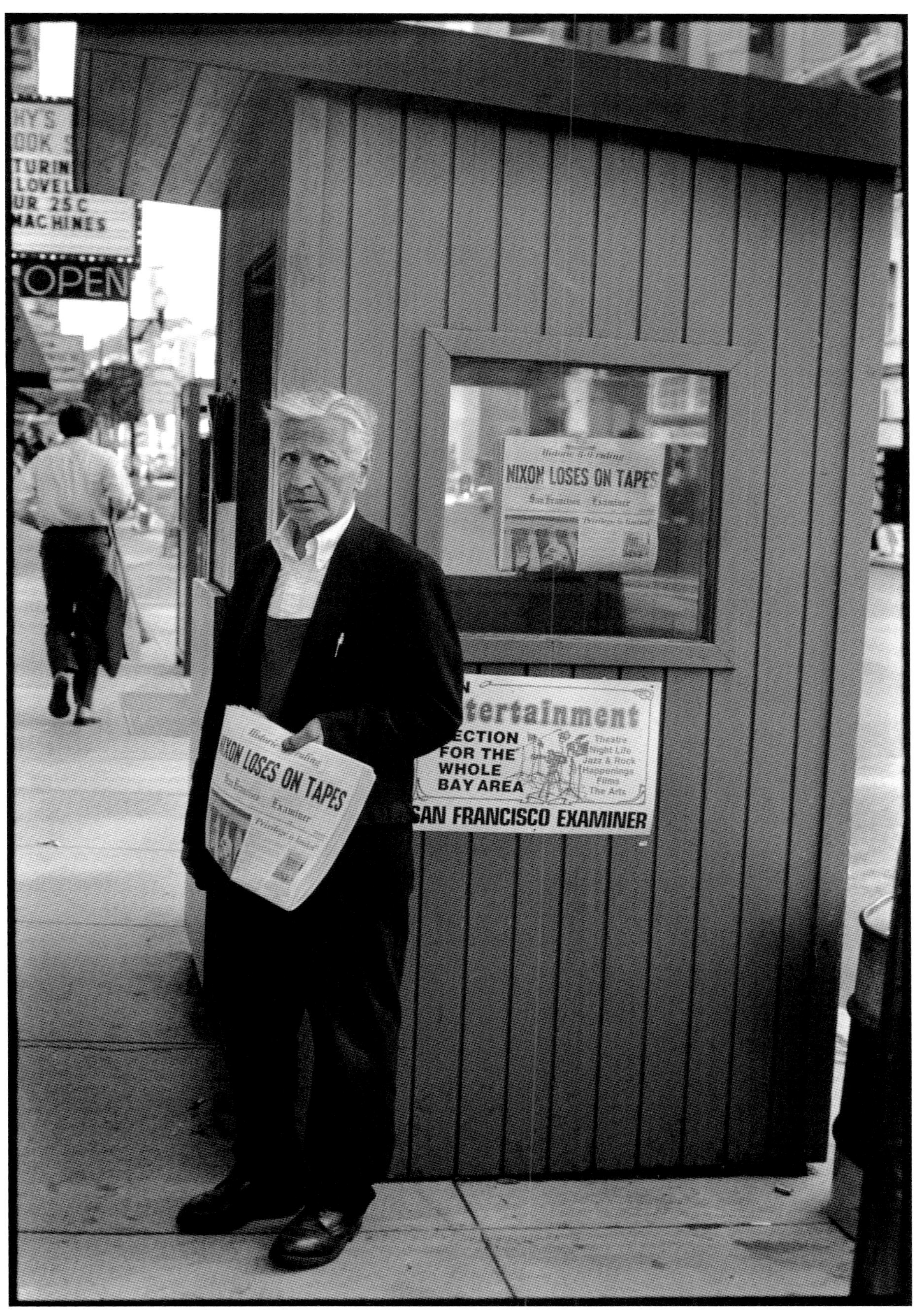

Nixon Loses Tapes, 1974
San Francisco, CA

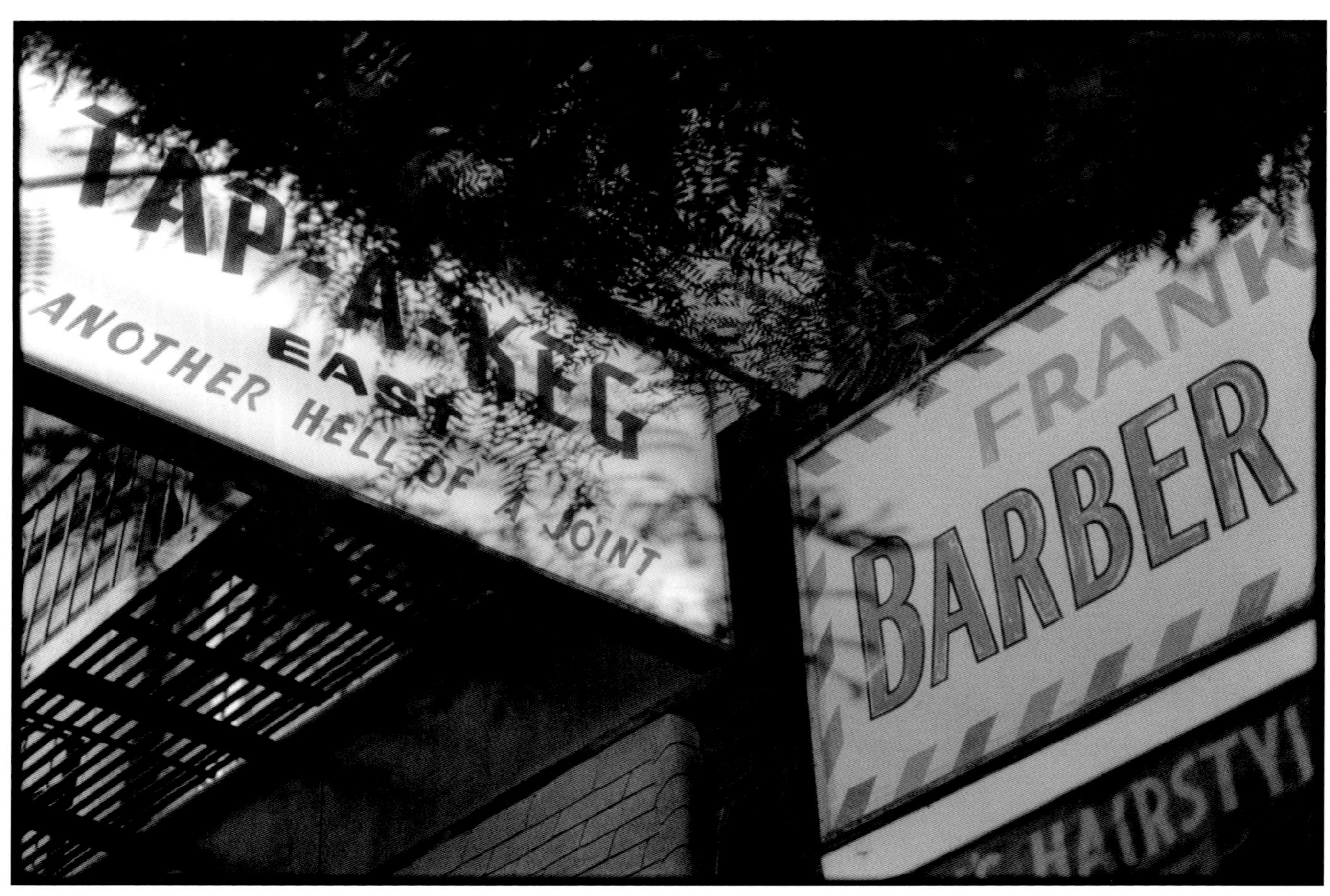

Hell of a Joint, 1984
New York, NY

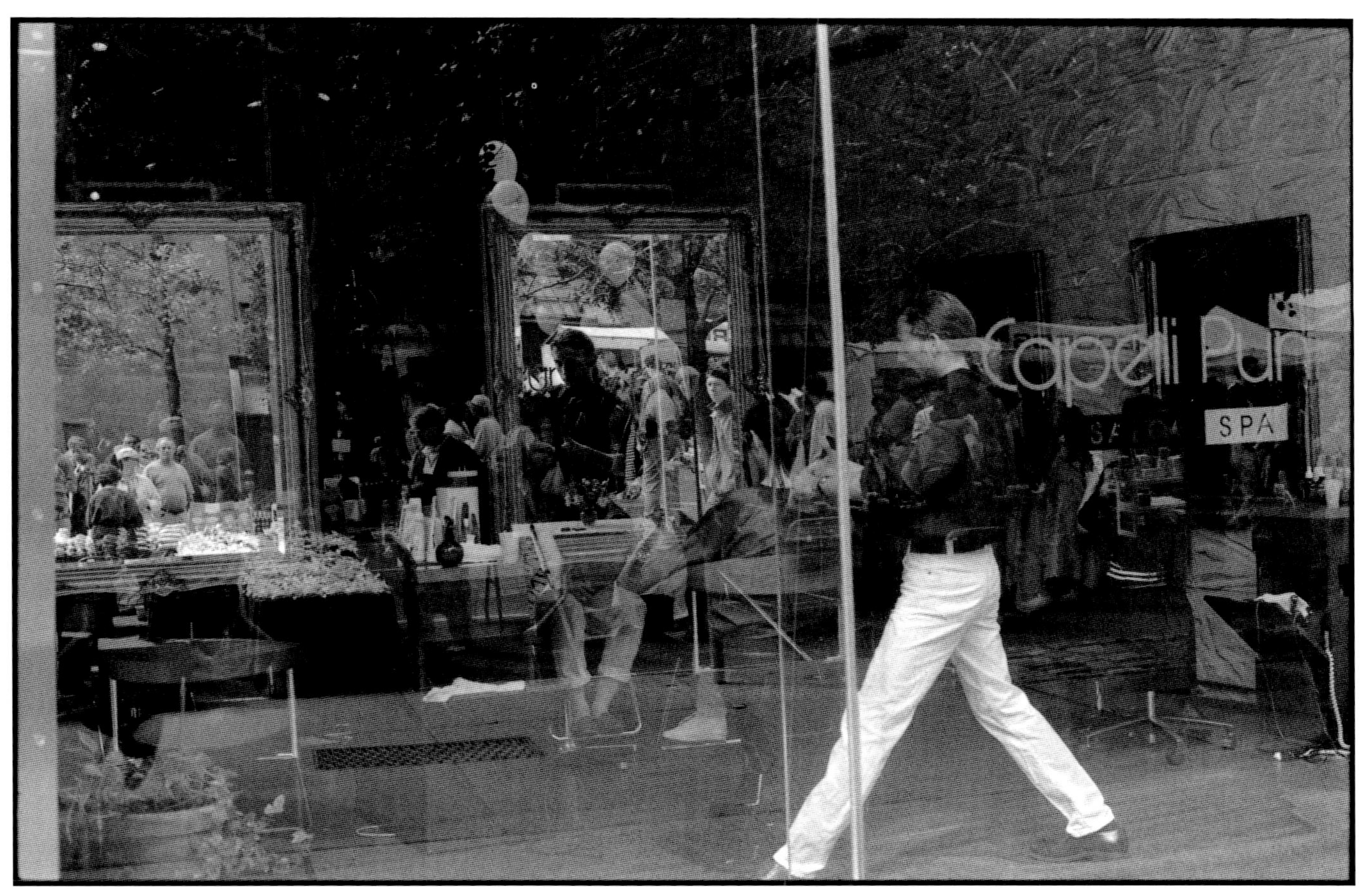

Pun Spa, 1996
New York, NY

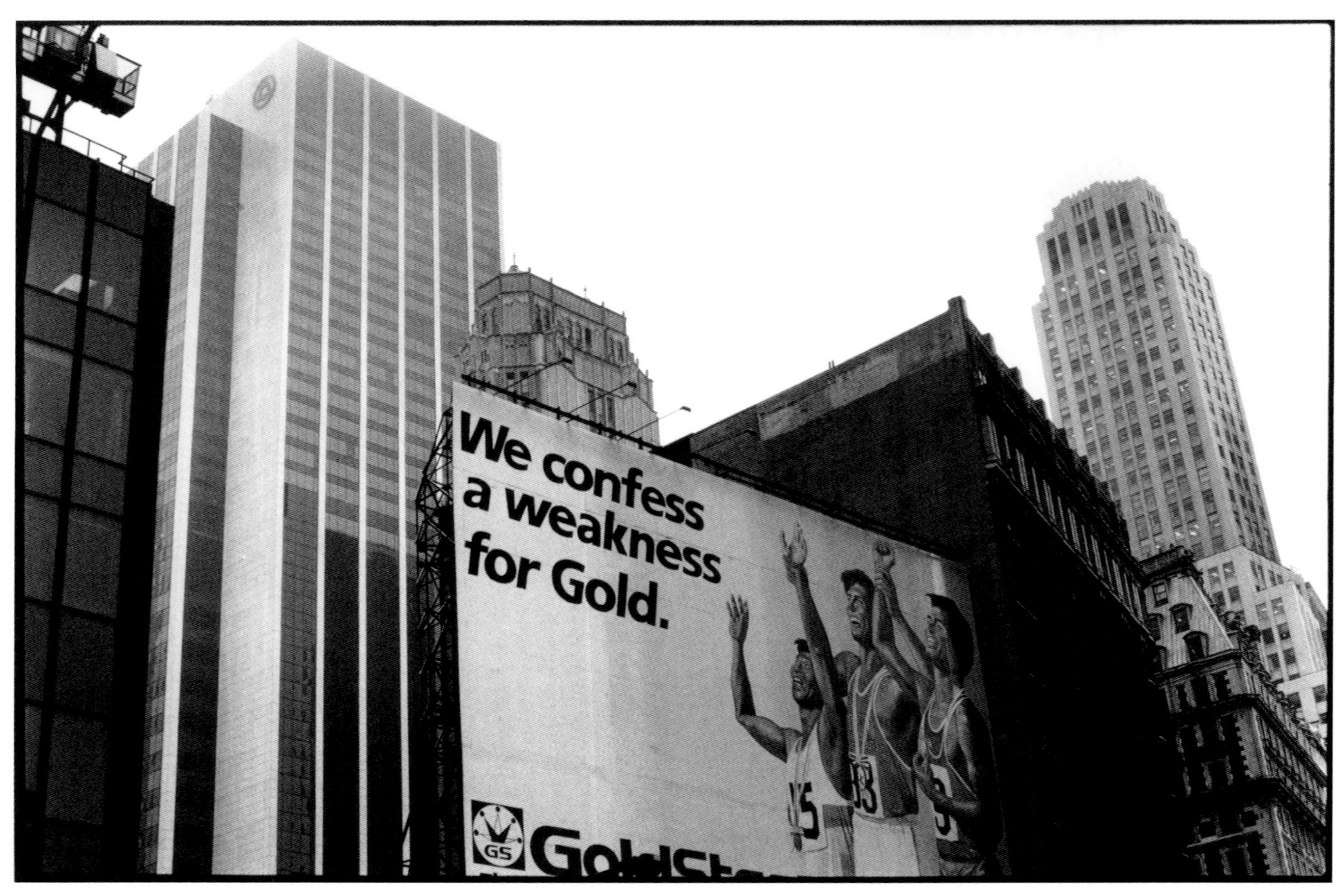

A Weakness for Gold, 1989
New York, NY

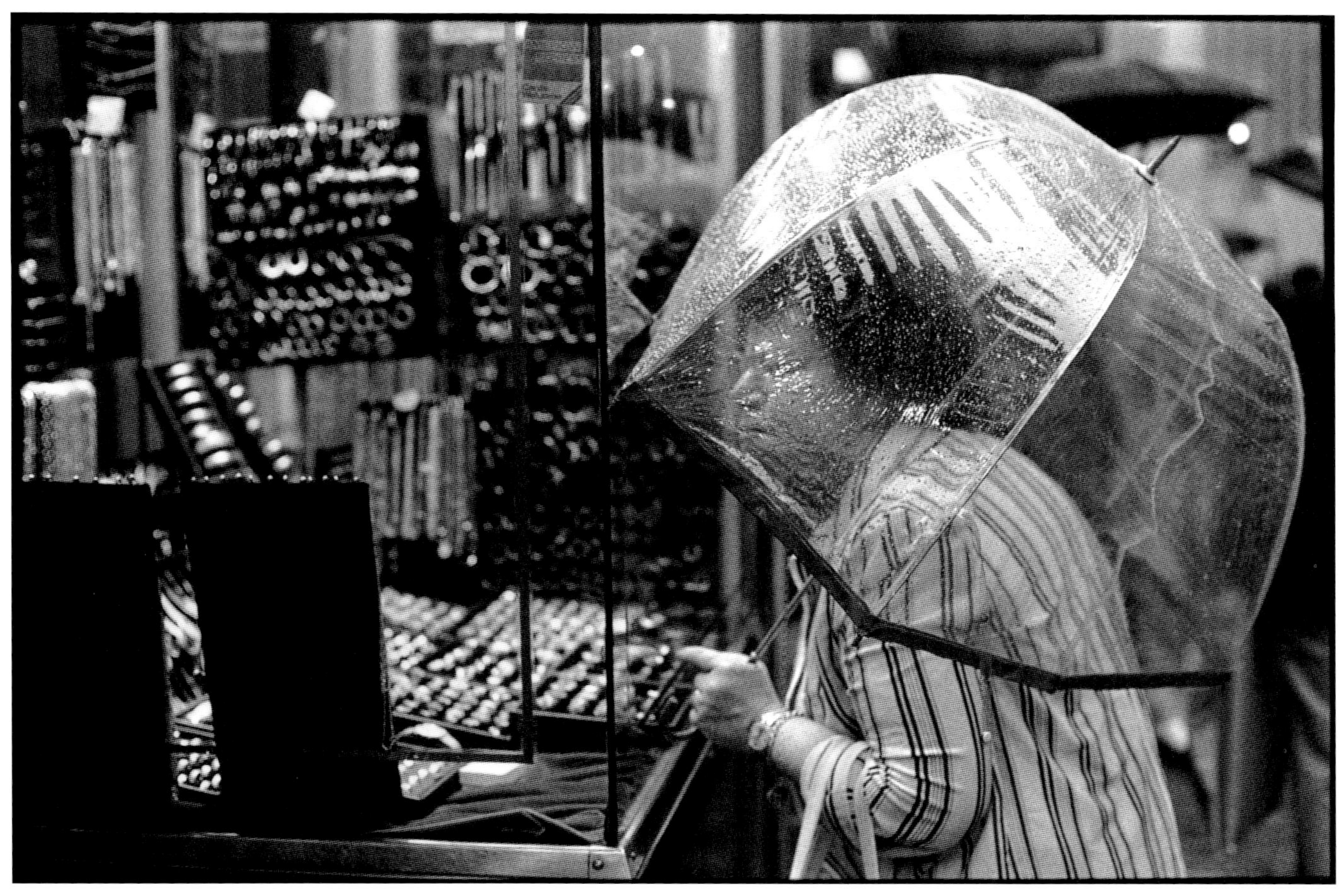

Diamond Lust, 1976
New York, NY

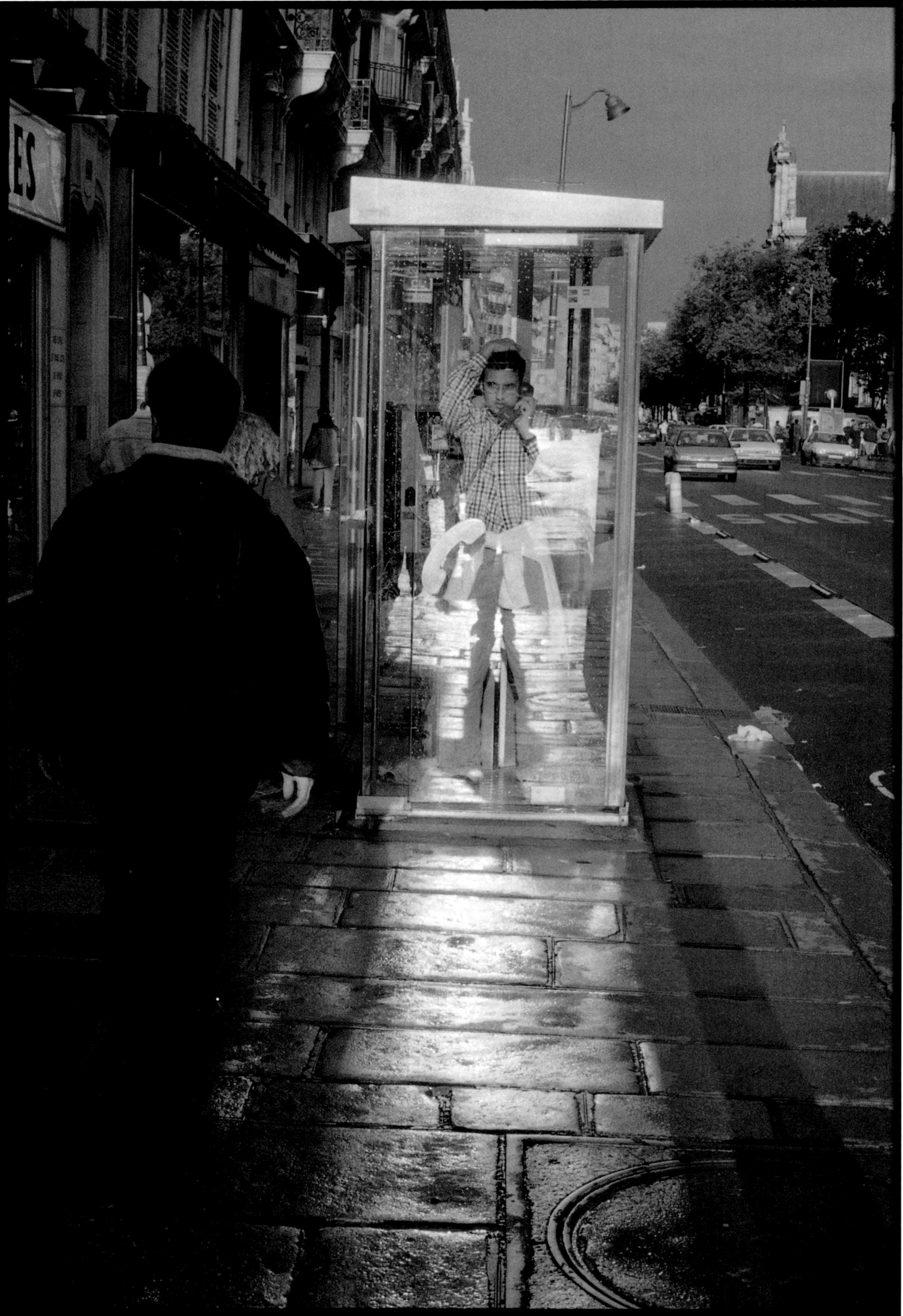

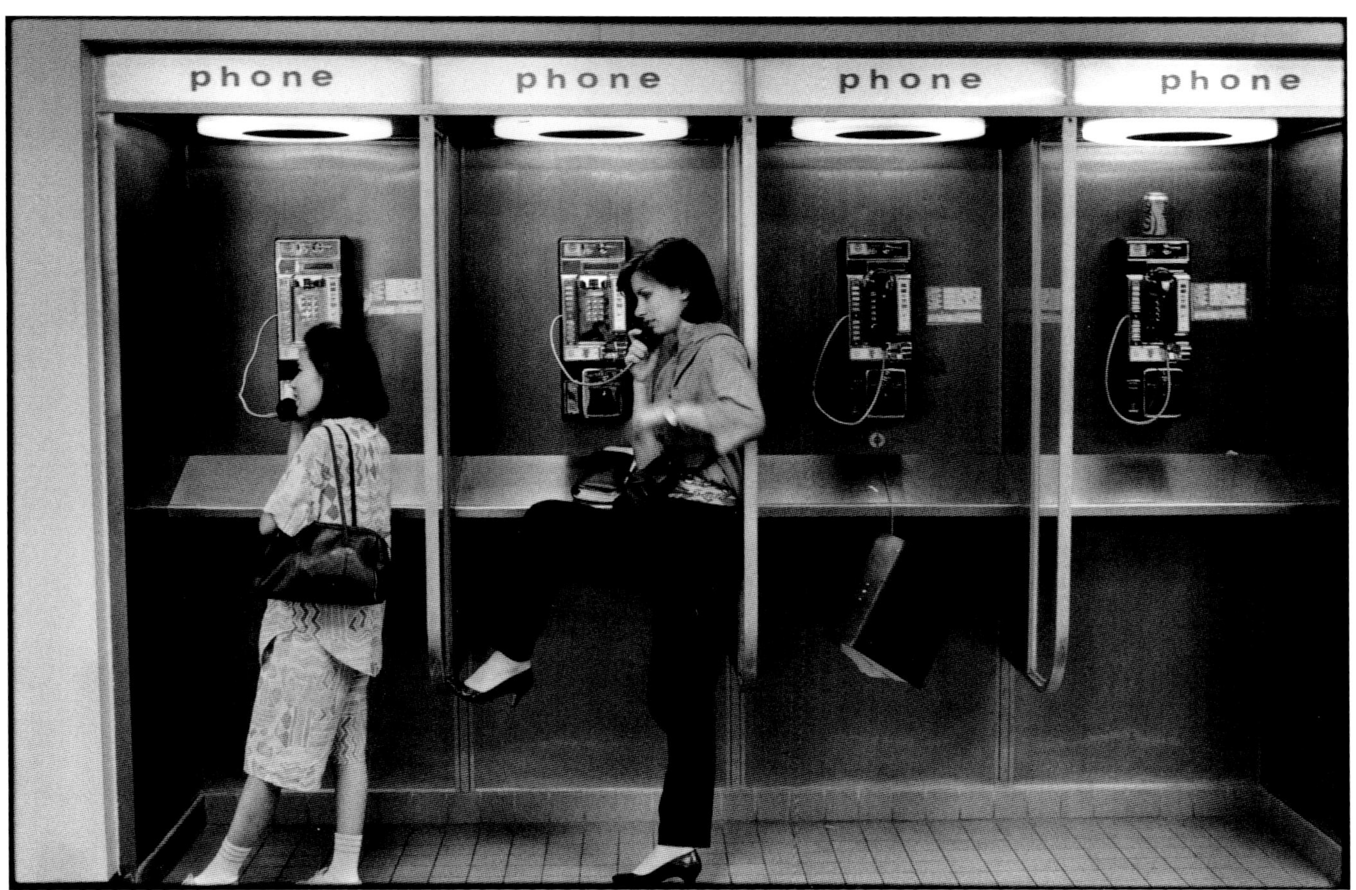

The Chat, 1989
New Orleans, LA

Beam Me Up Scotty, 1997
St-Germain-des-Prés, Paris, France

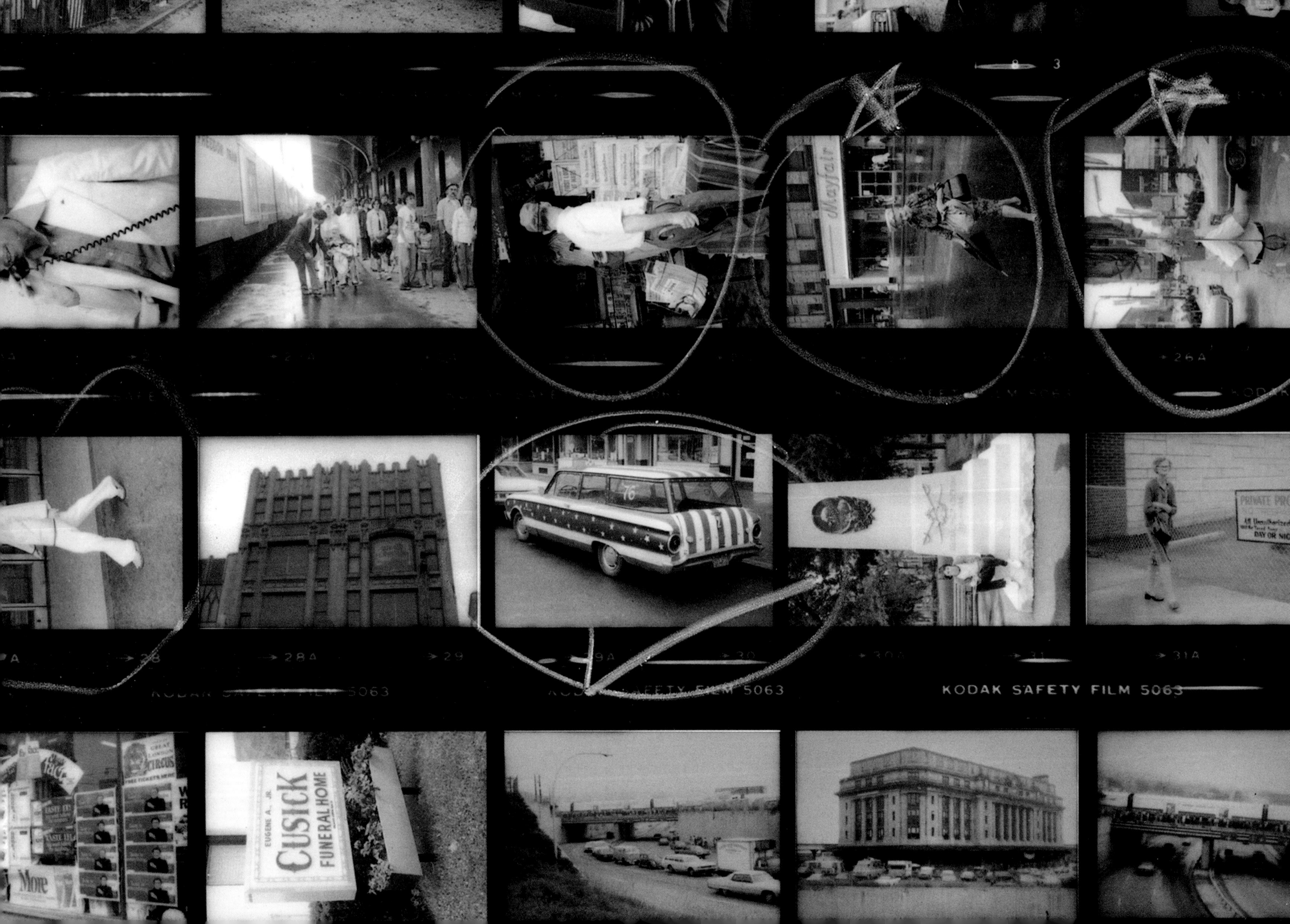

KODAK SAFETY FILM 5063
KODAK SAFETY FILM 5063
Mayfair
EUGENE A., JR.
CUSICK
FUNERAL HOME
More
PRIVATE PR
DAY OR NIG
76

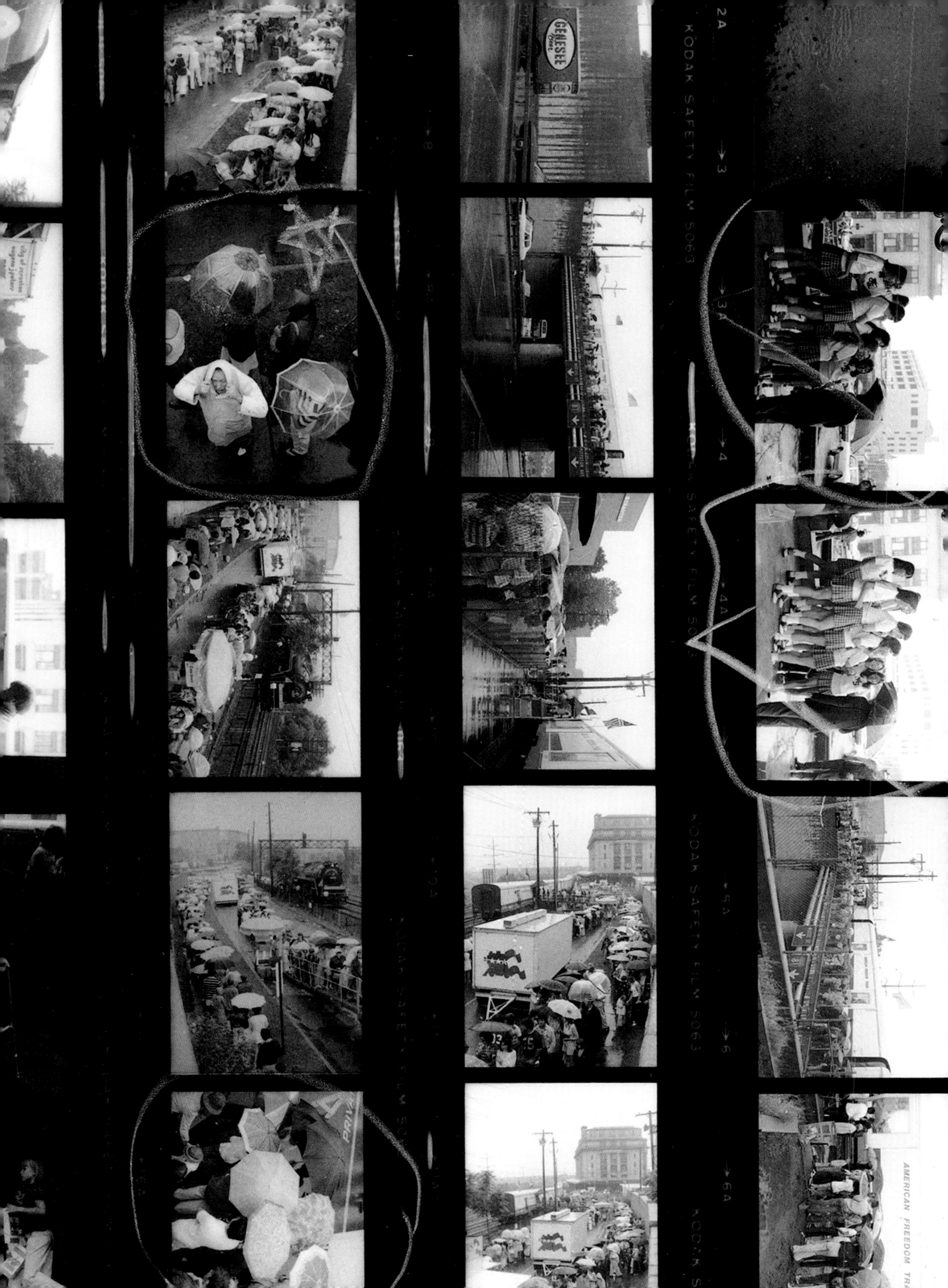

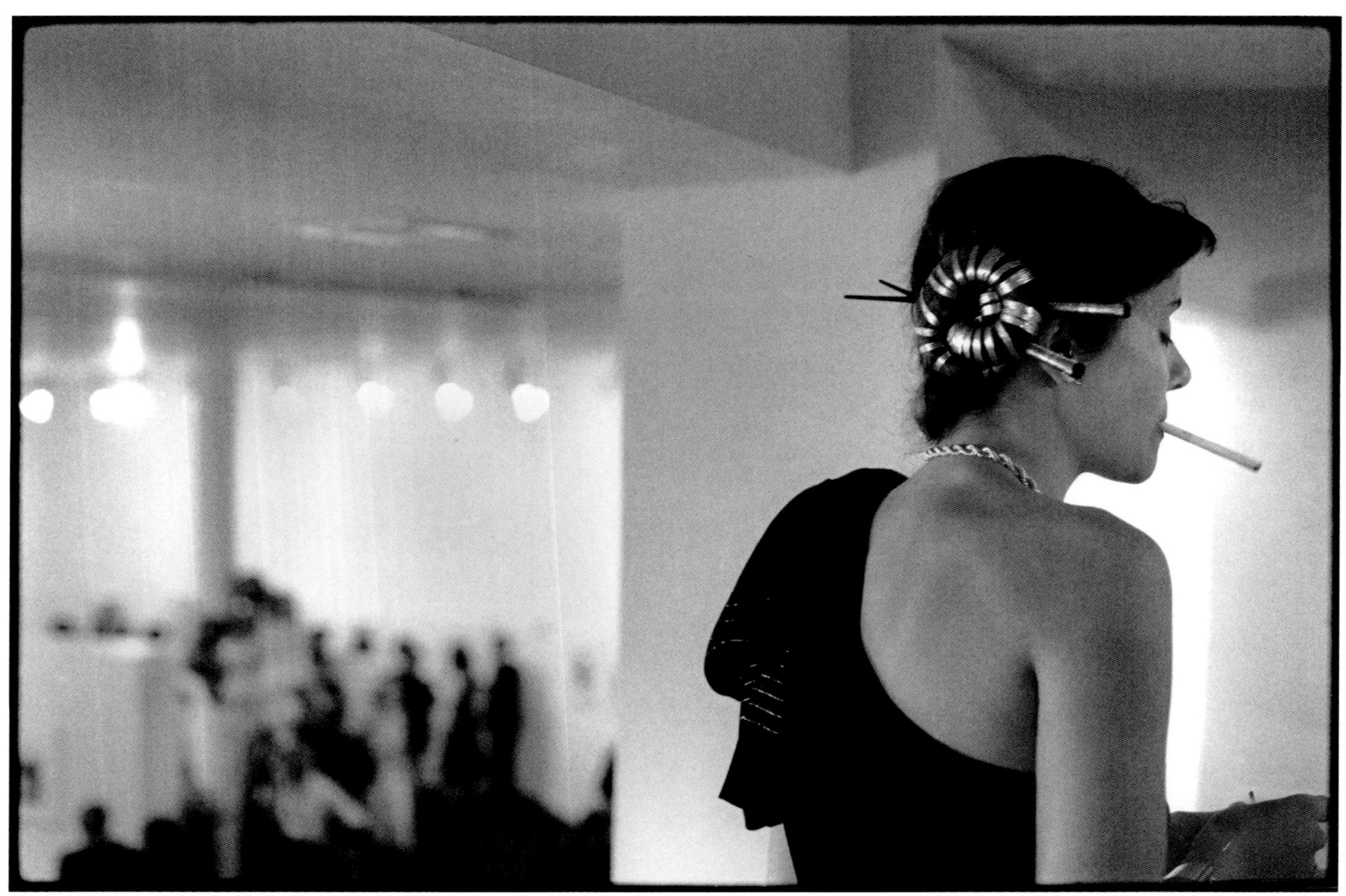

InElegant Cigarette, 1980
Washington, DC

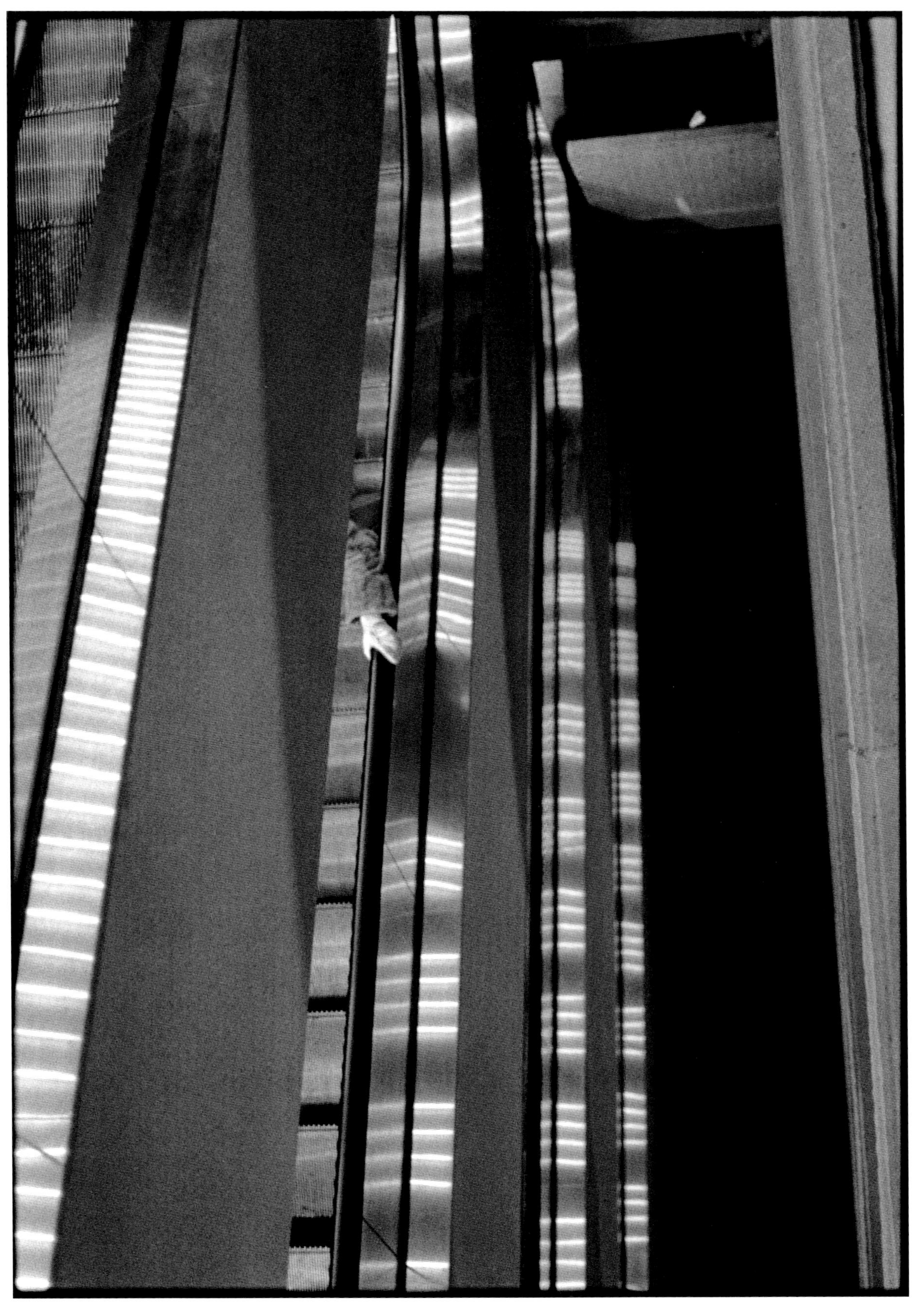

The Mall, 1979
Atlanta, GA

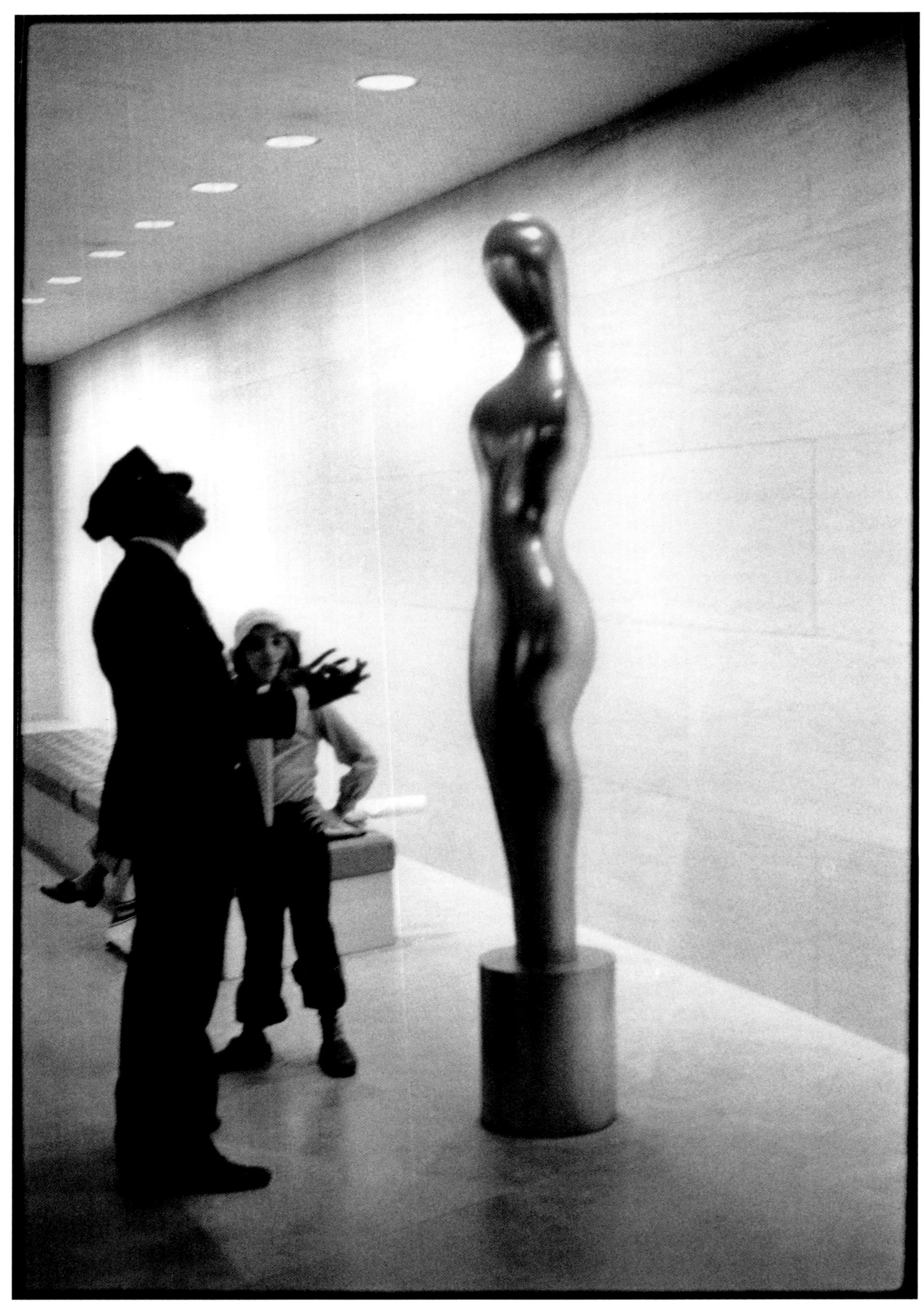

Guard Teaching Art, The National Gallery, 1978
Washington, DC

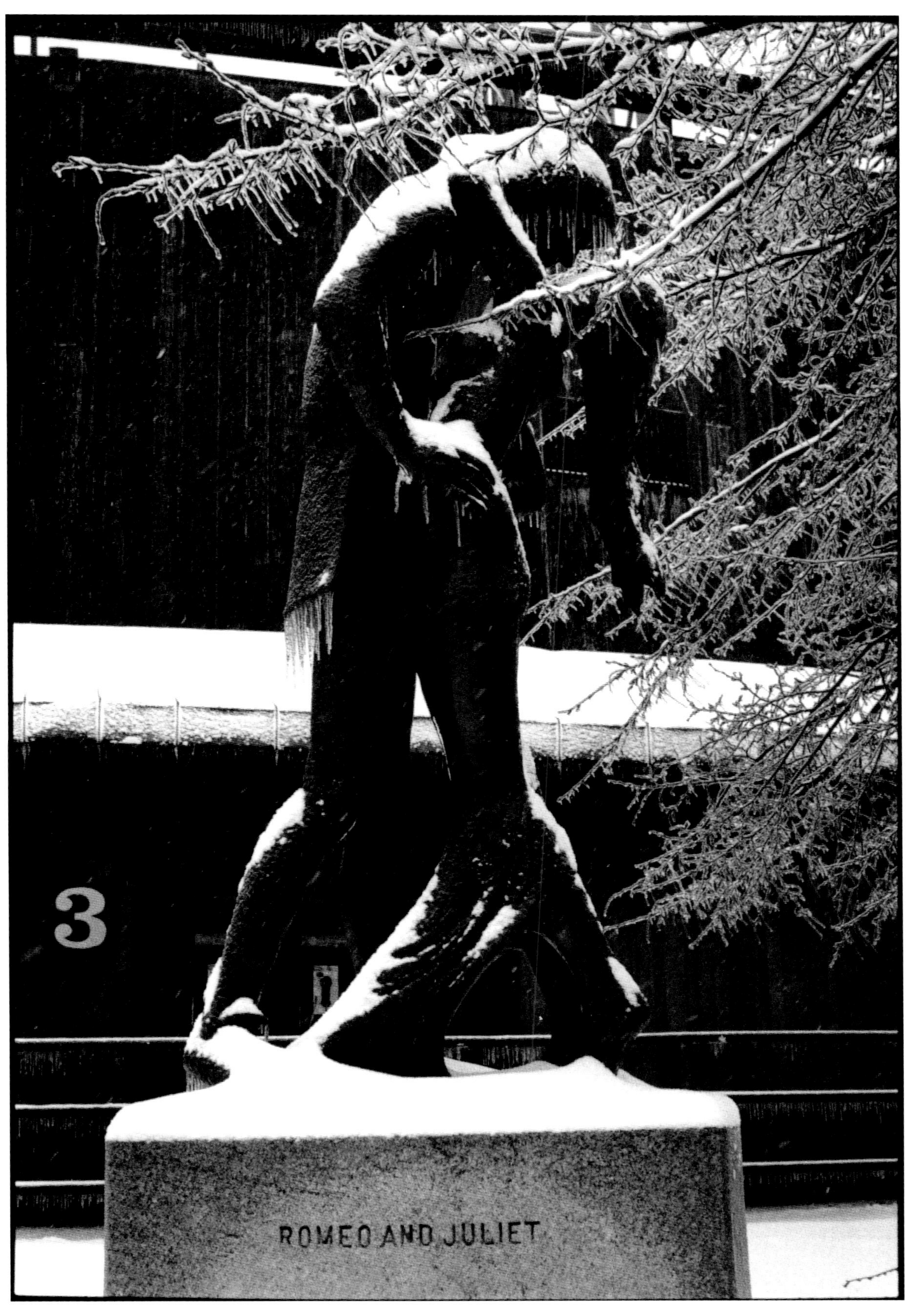

Frozen Love, 1990
New York, NY

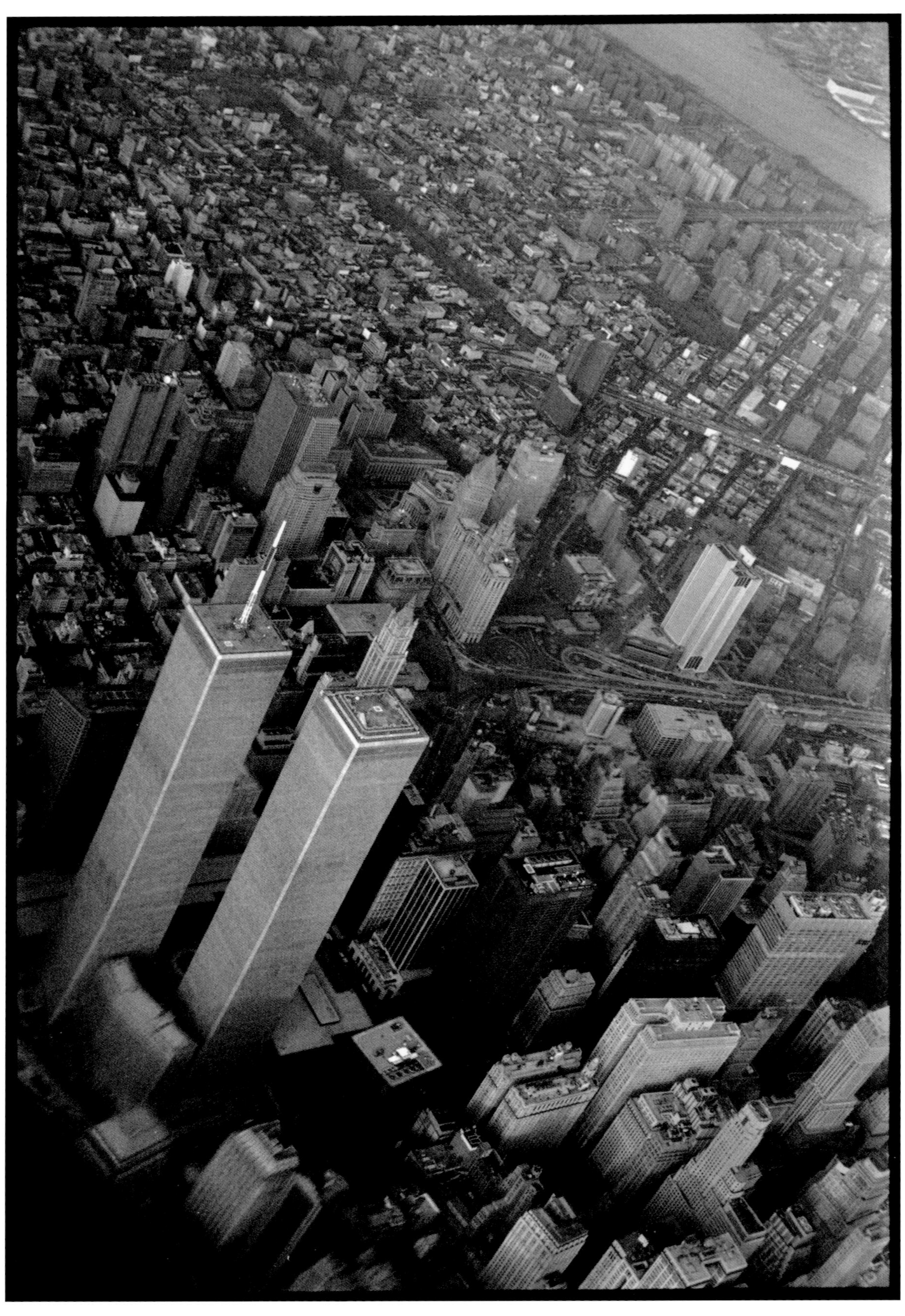

New York City, 1988
New York, NY

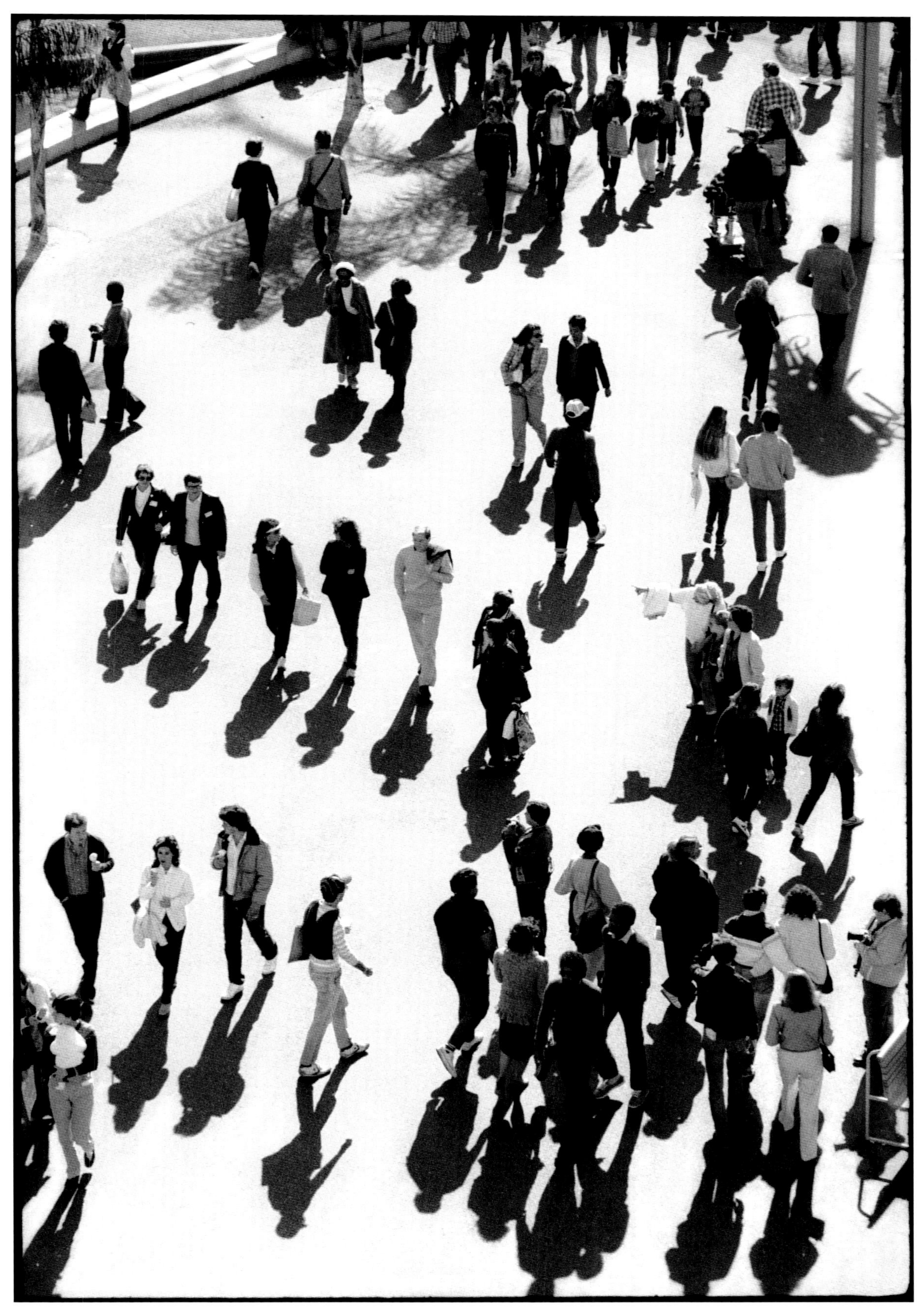

Shadow People, 1984
New Orleans, LA

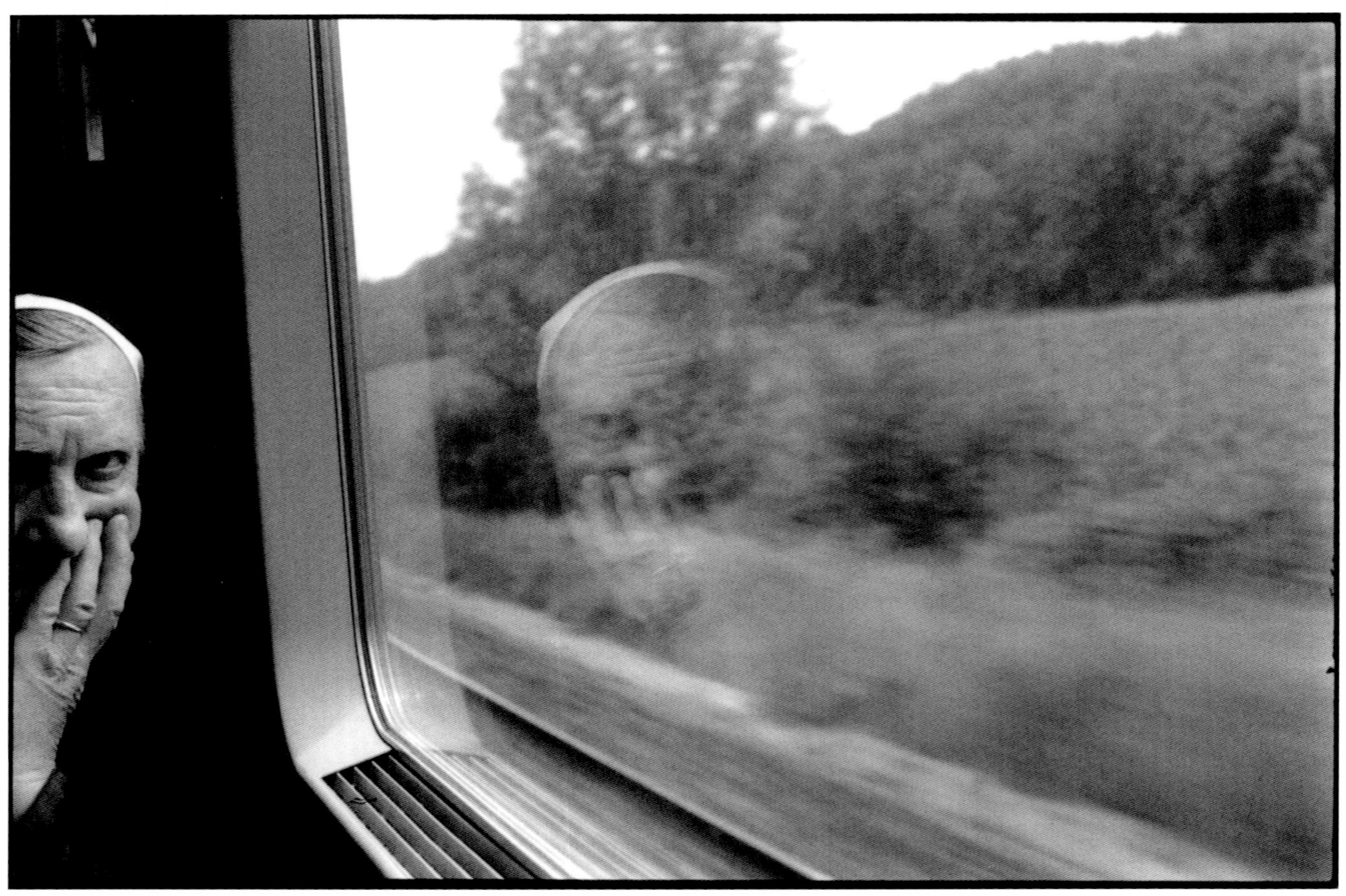

Journey to Eternity, 1990
Paris to Zurich

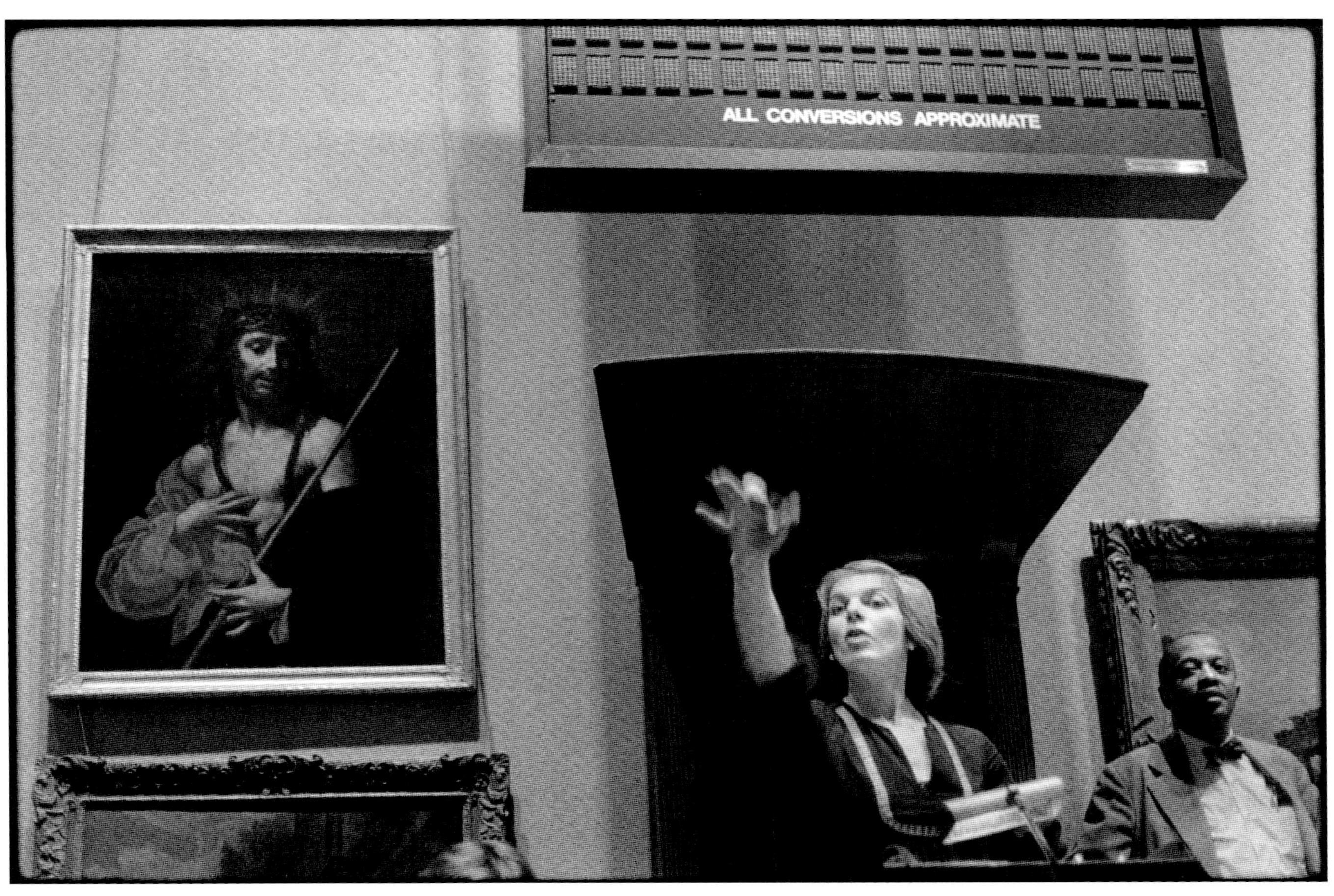

All Conversions Approximate, 1978
New York, NY

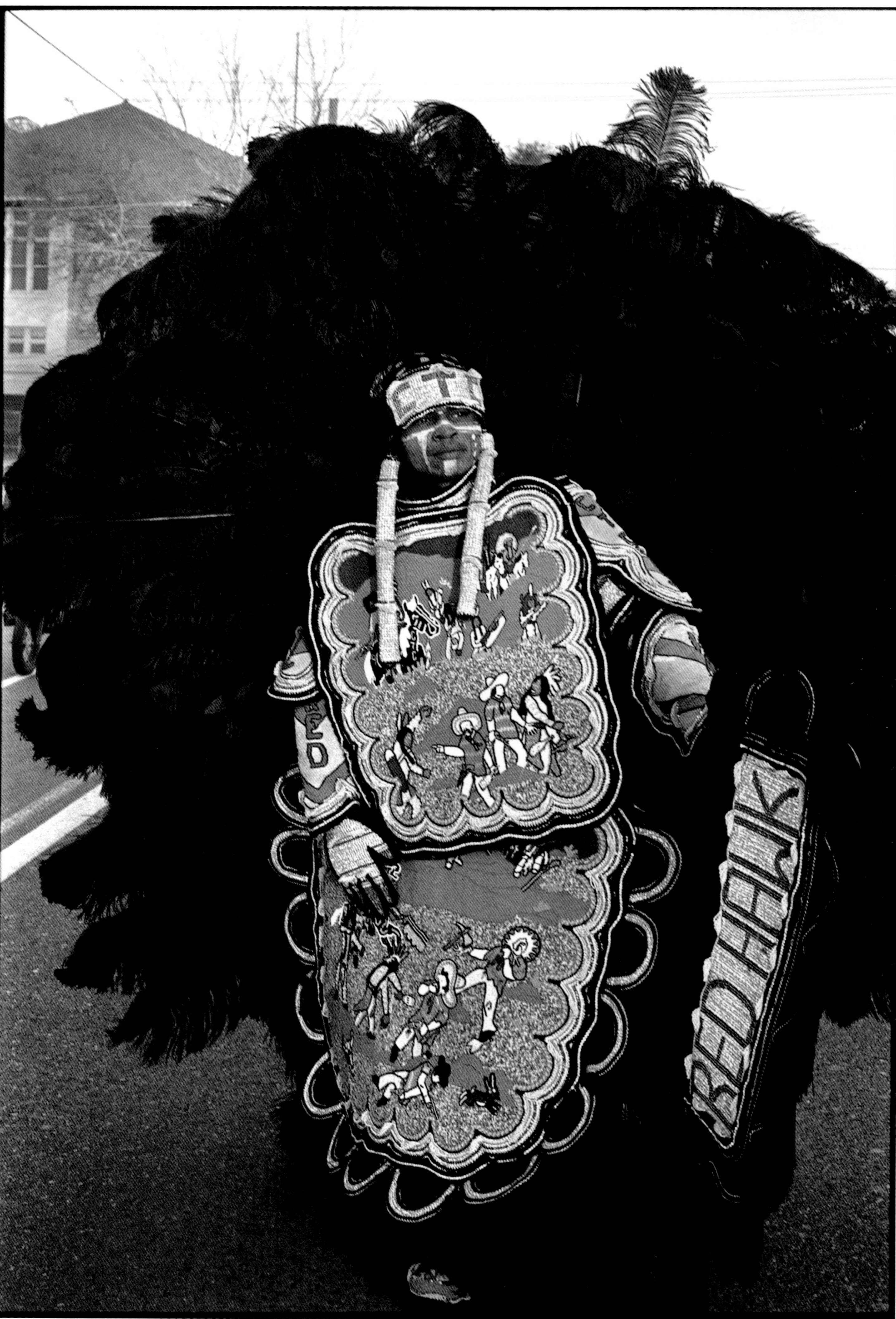
RED HAWK

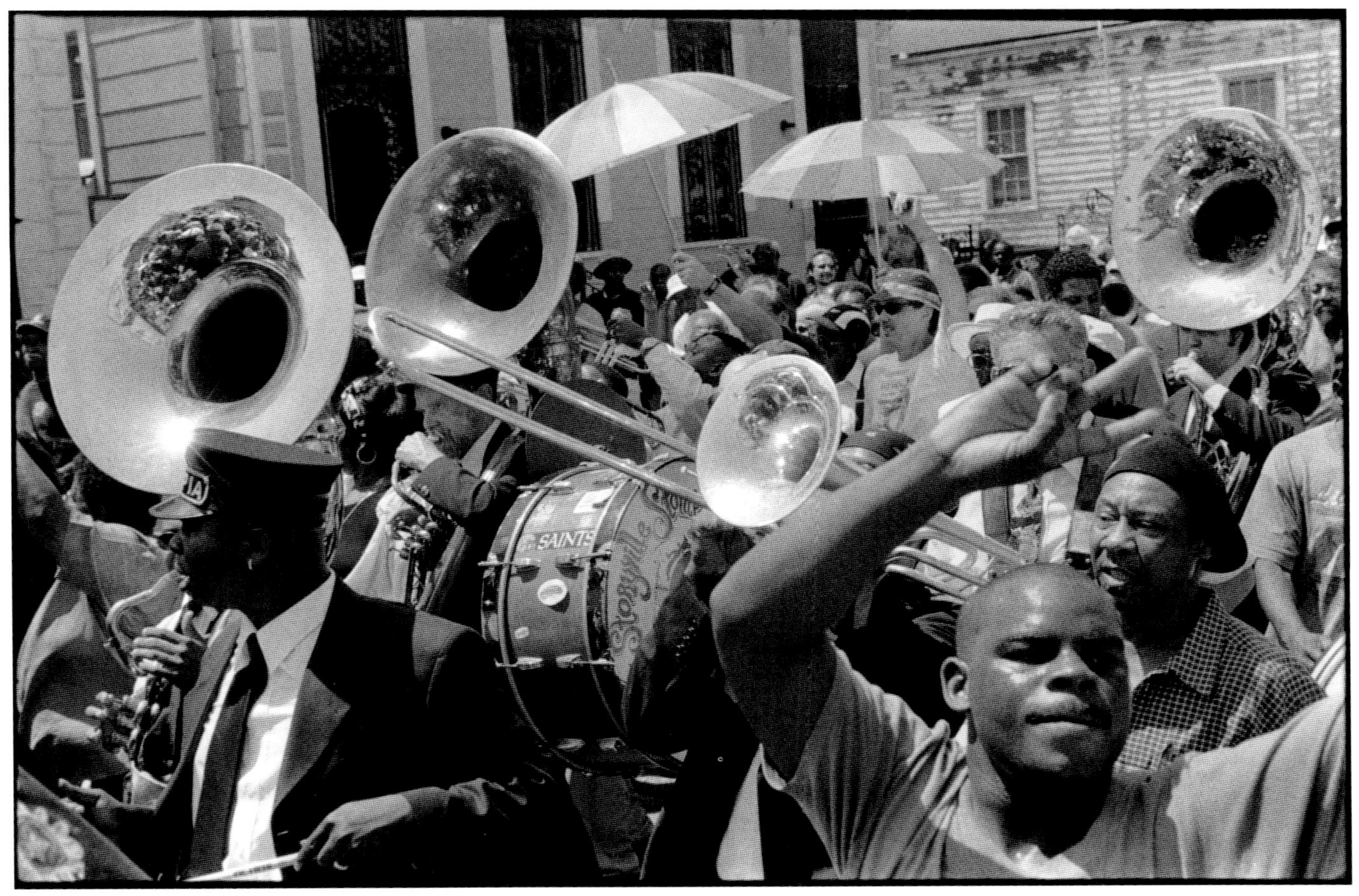

Second Line, 2001
New Orleans, LA

Red Hawk, Mardi Gras Indian, 2009
New Orleans, LA

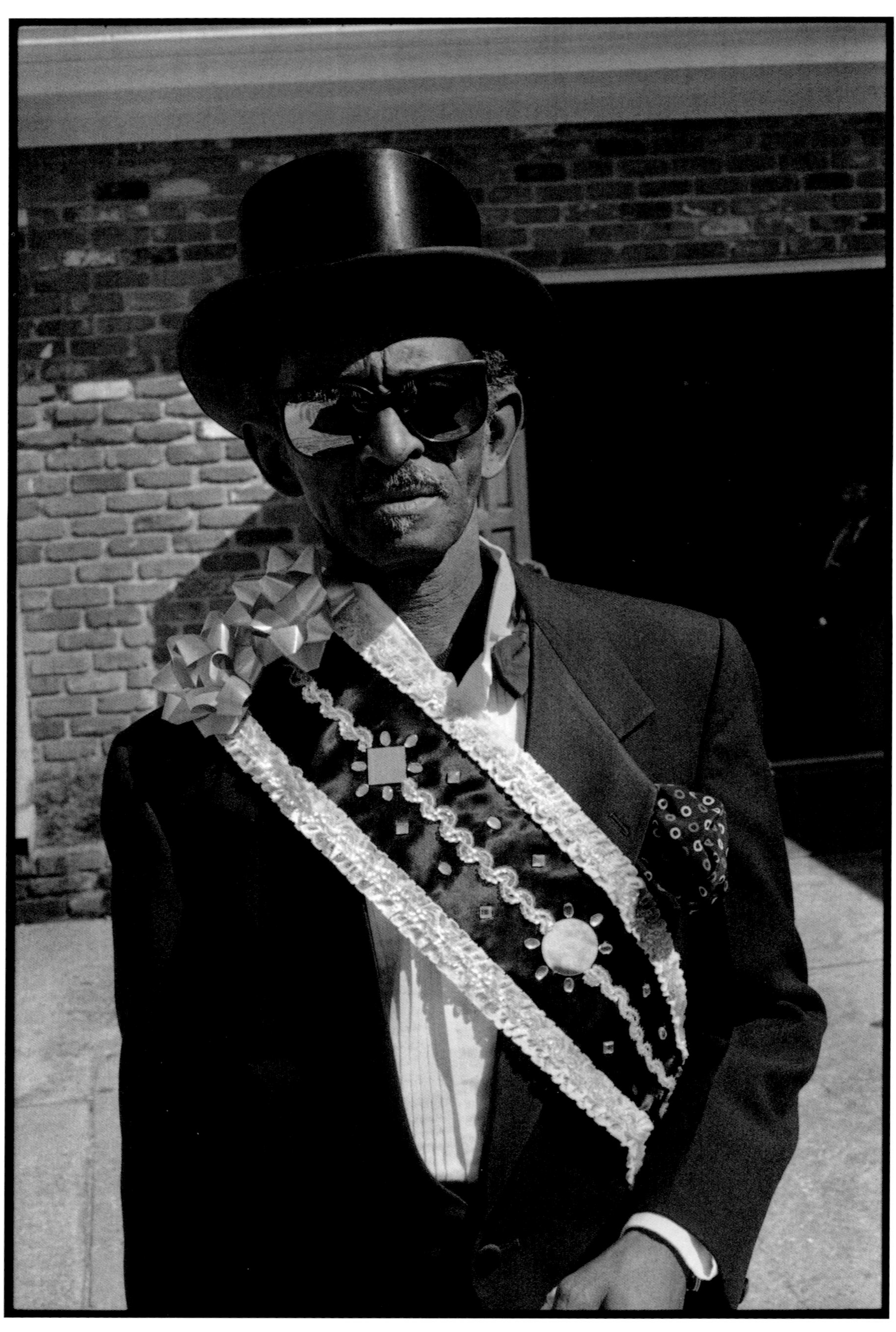

"Uncle" Lionel Batiste, 1990
New Orleans, LA

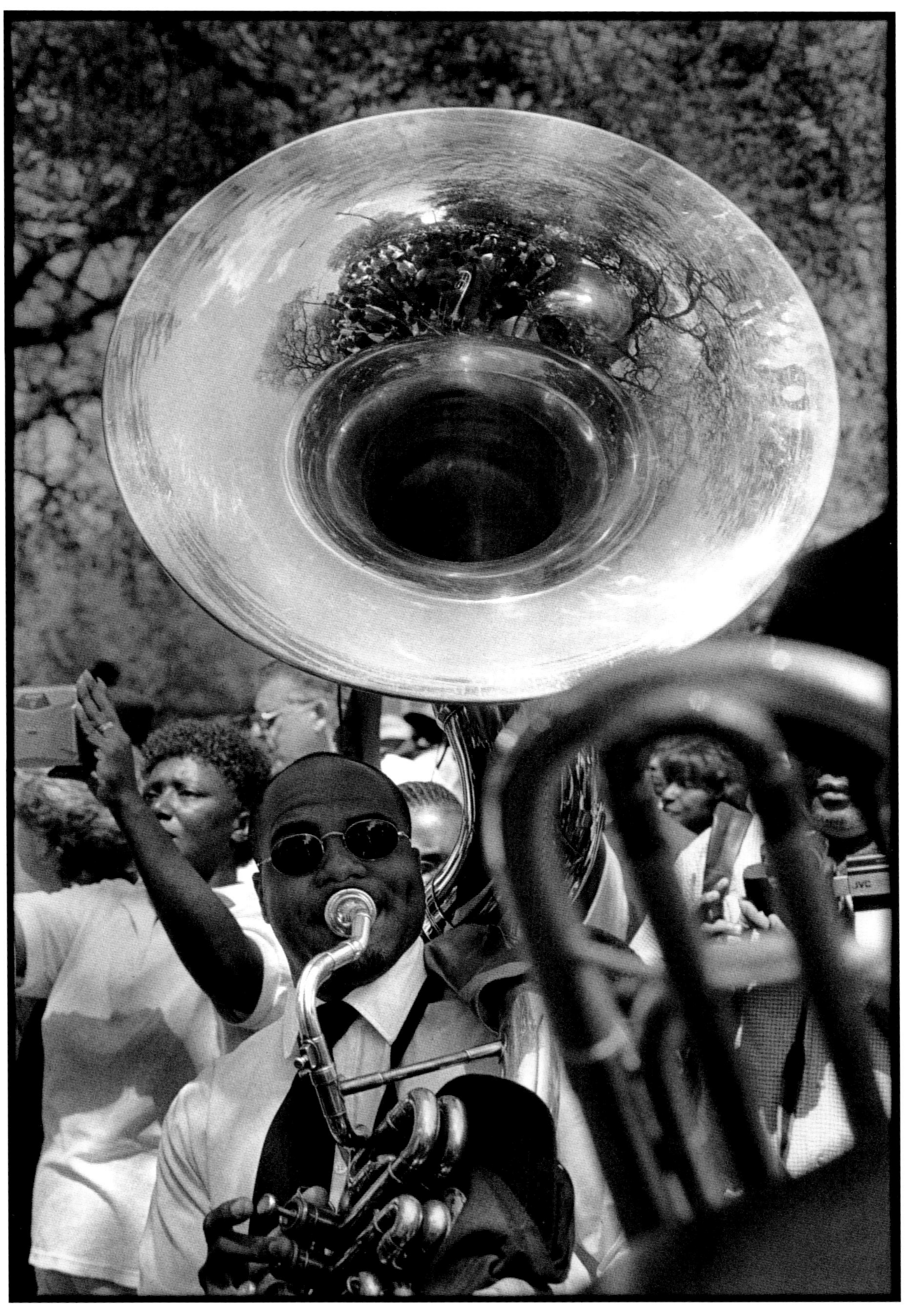

Sounds of Music, 2001
New Orleans, LA

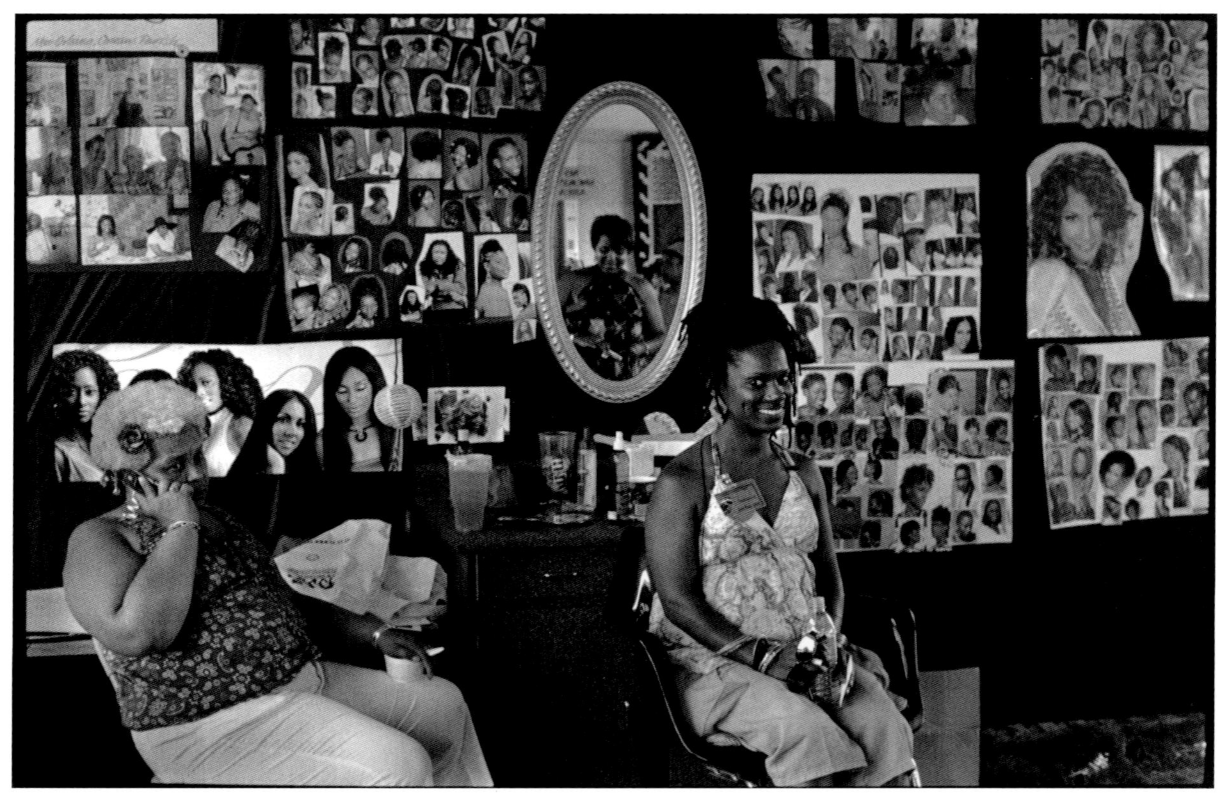

Hair, 2000
New Orleans, LA

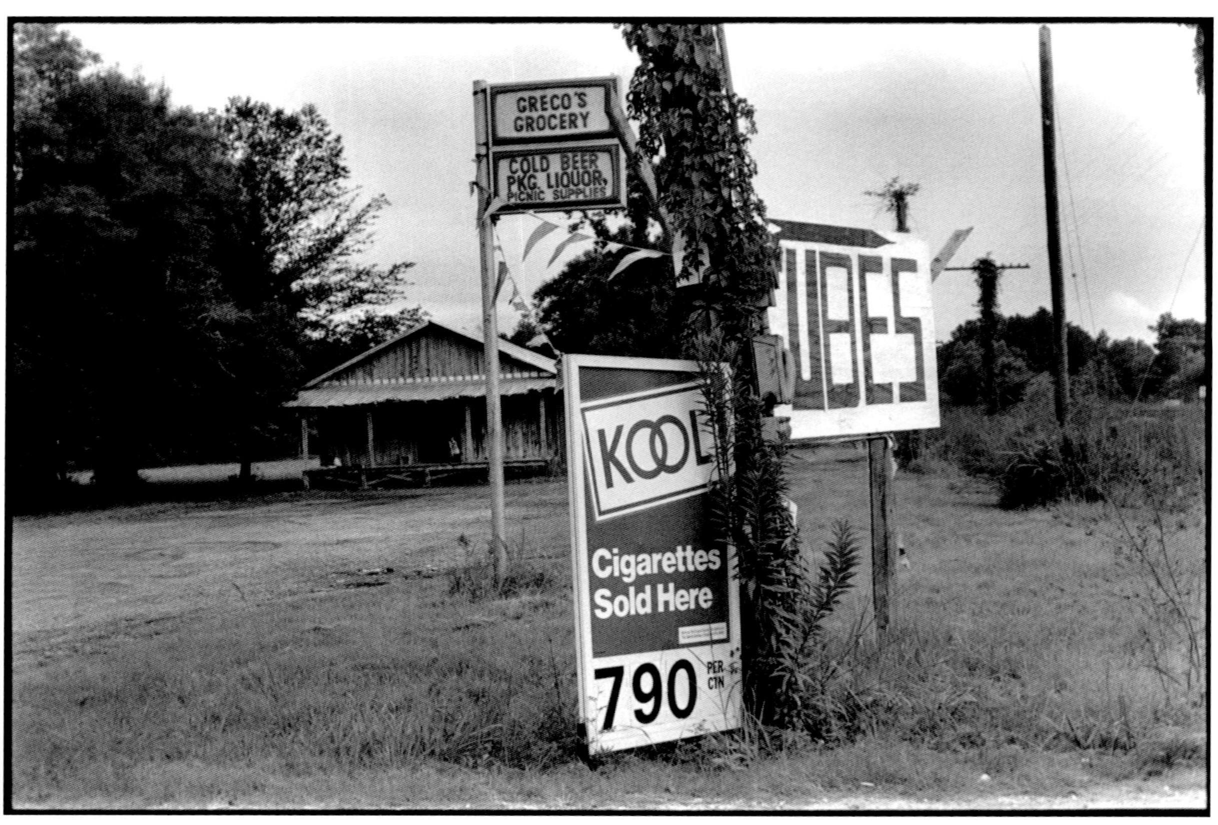

Greco's Grocery, 1983
Robert, LA

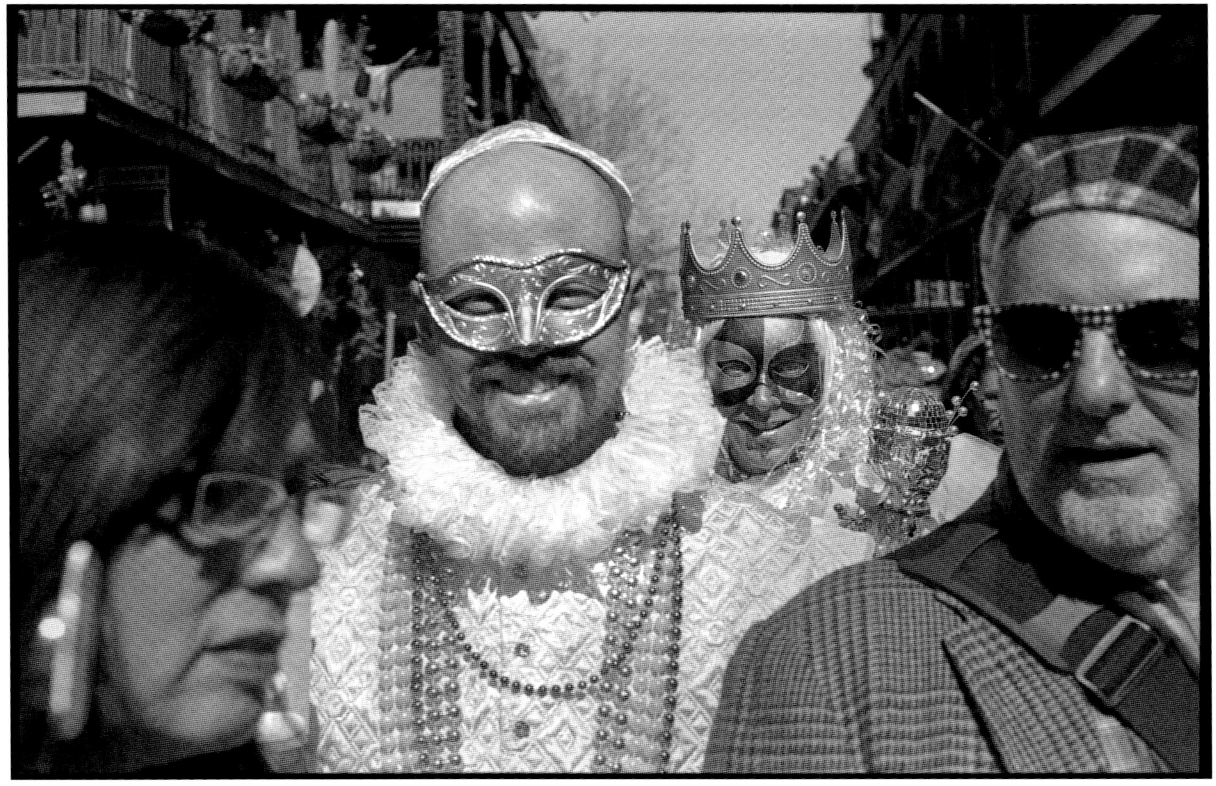

Mardi Gras, 2010
New Orleans, LA

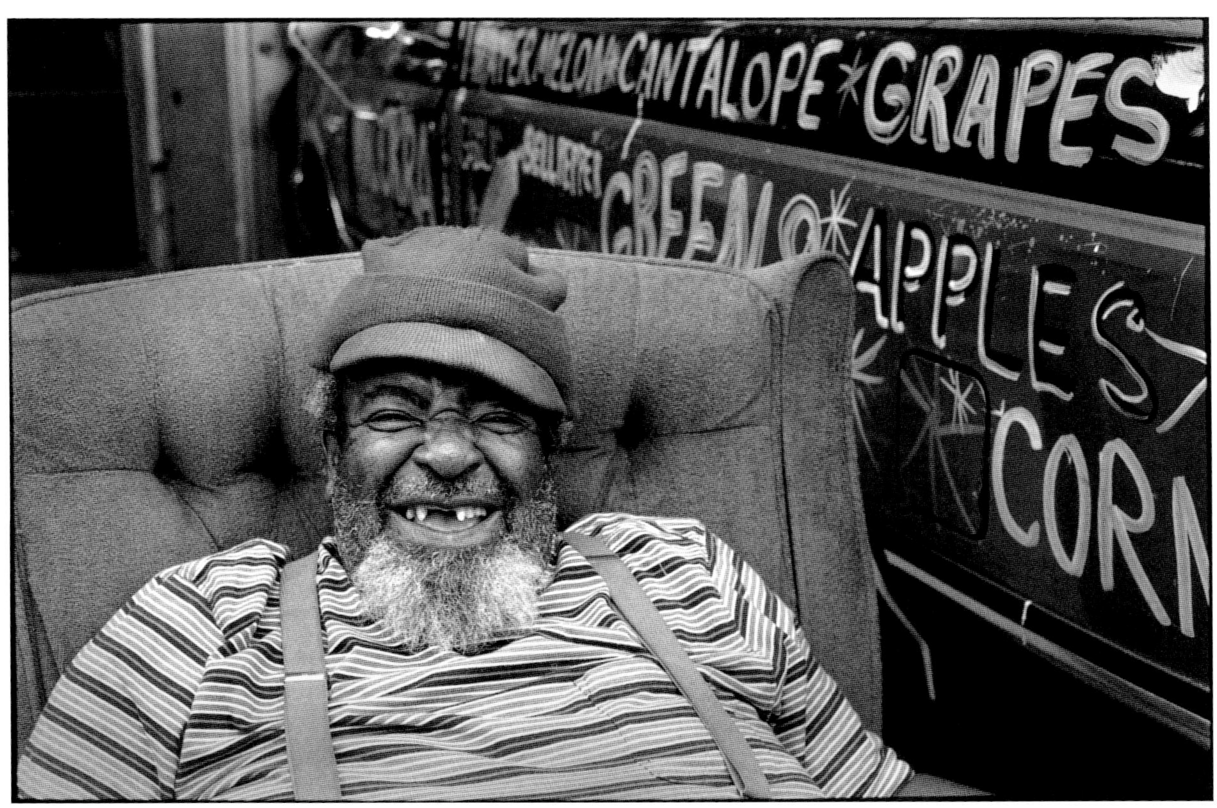

"Mr. Okra" Arthur Robinson, 2006
New Orleans, LA

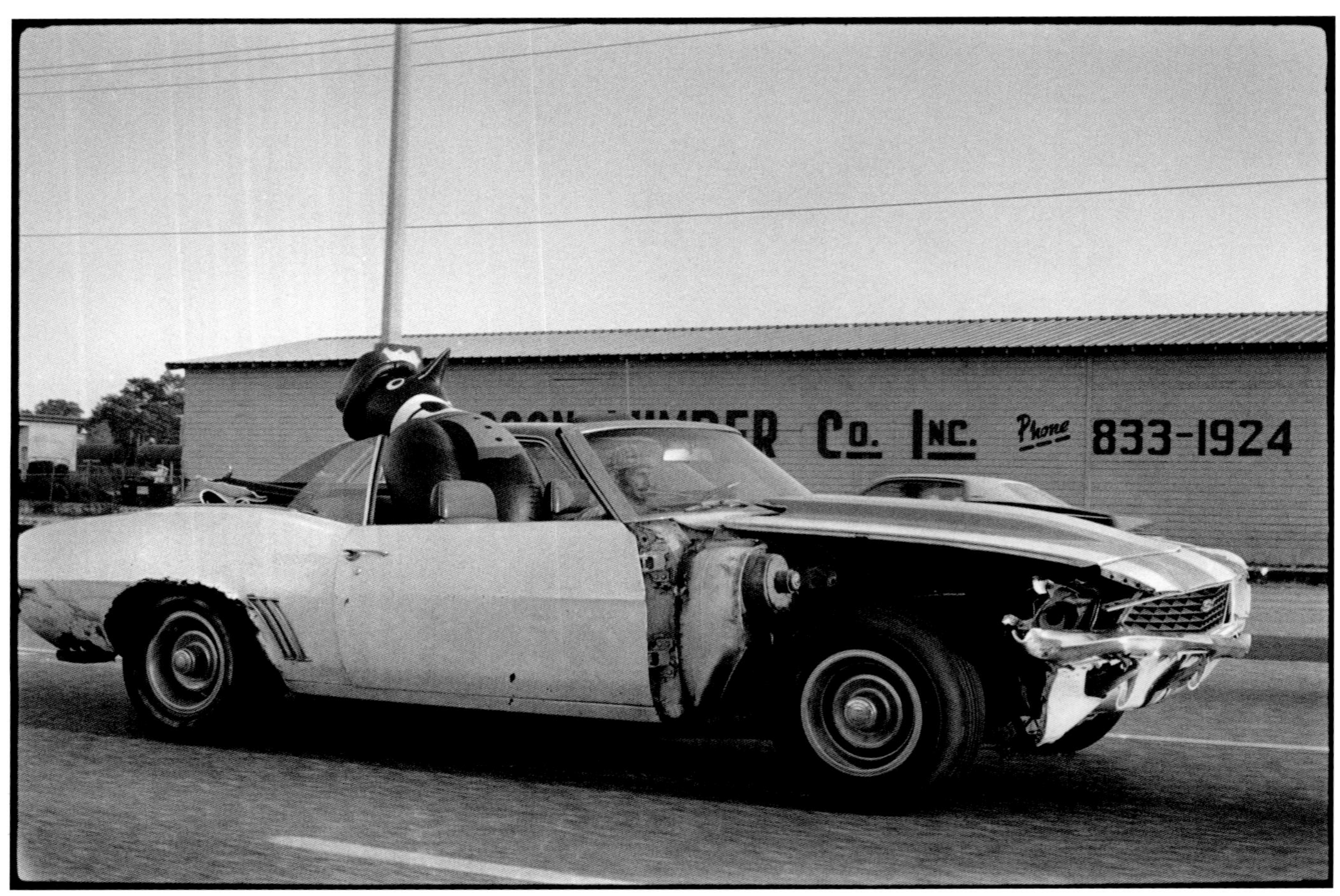

Company, Inc., 1977
New Orleans, LA

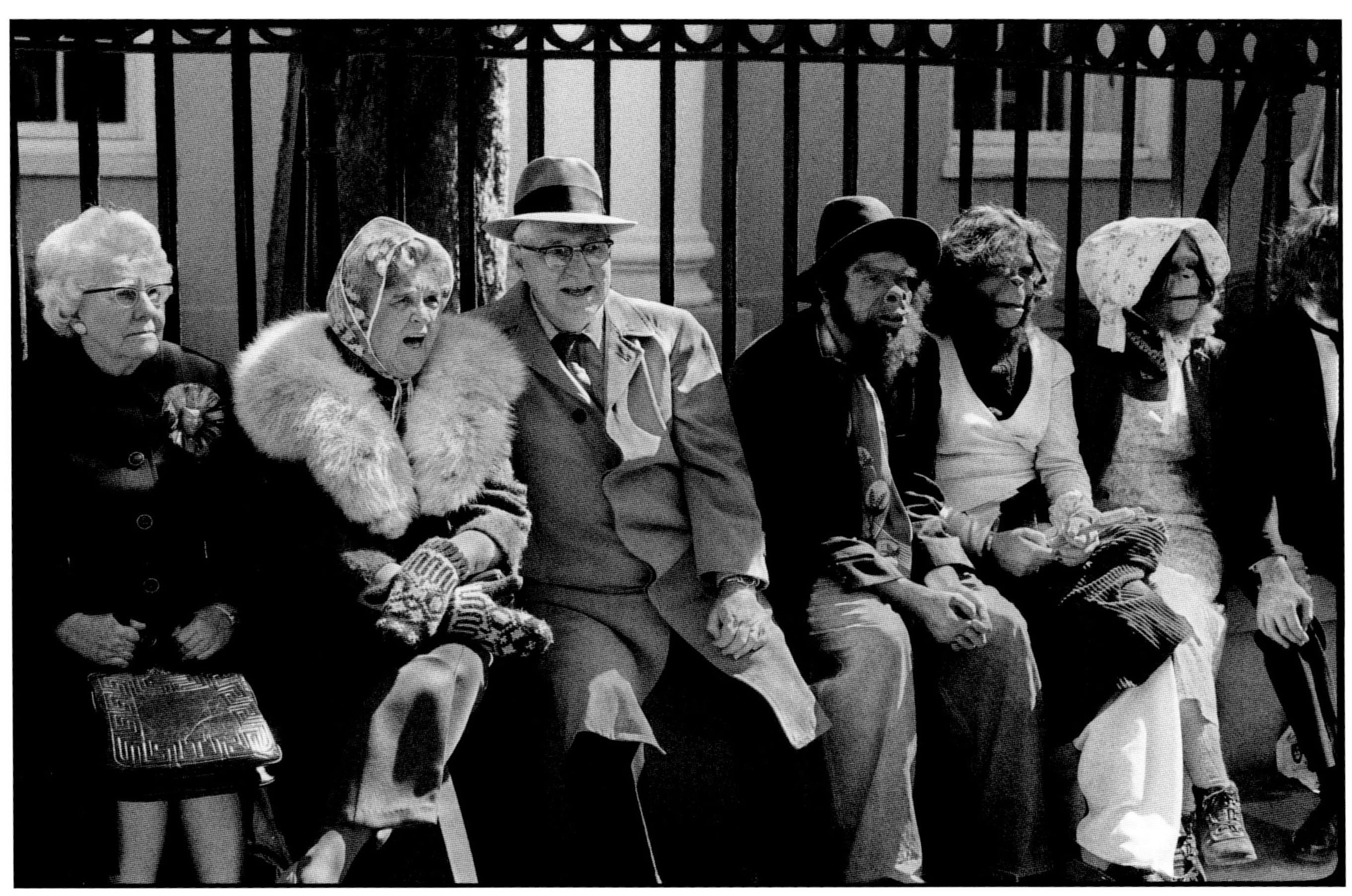

Man and Apes, 1974
New Orleans, LA

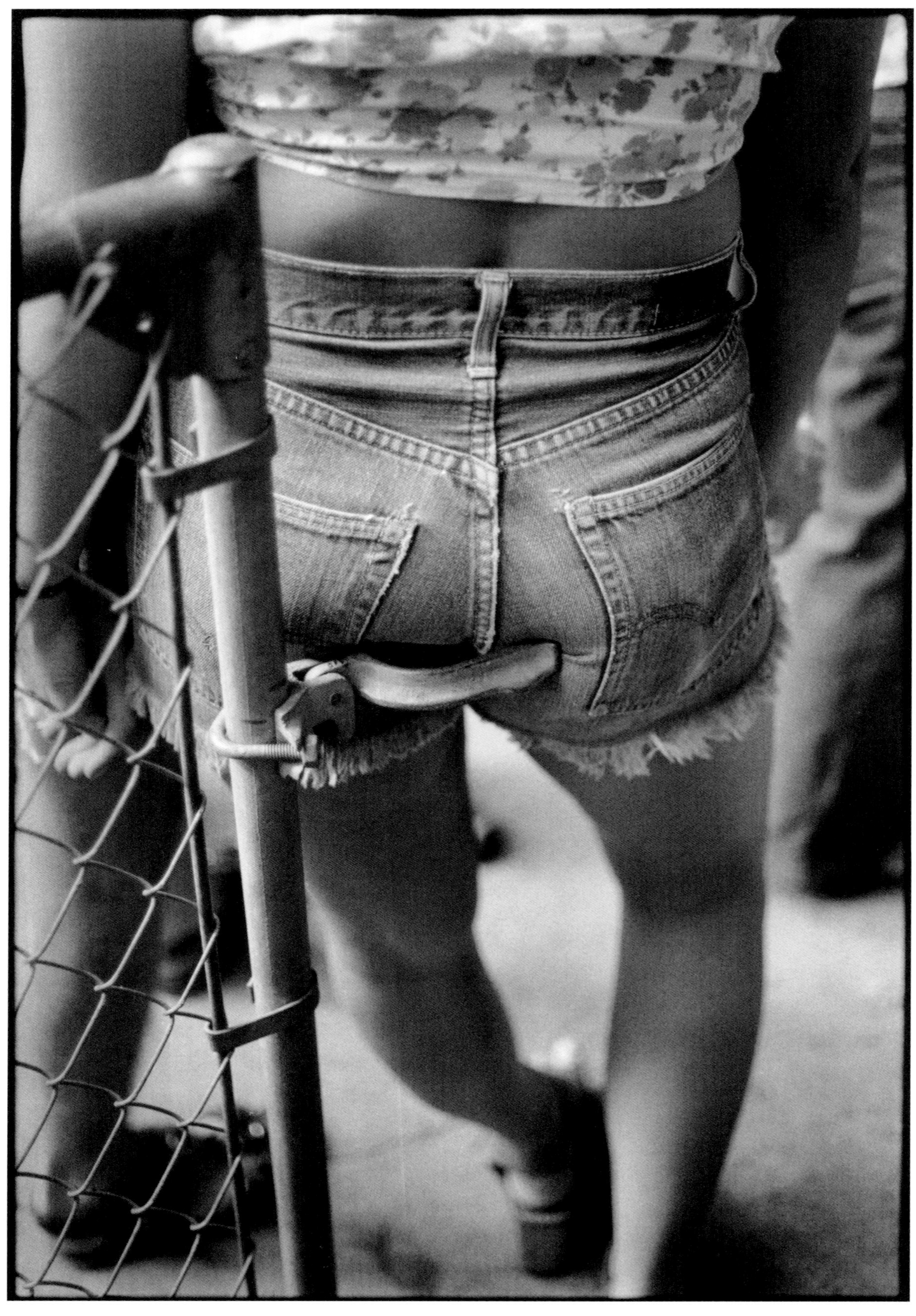

Don't Ask Me, 1974
Baton Rouge, LA

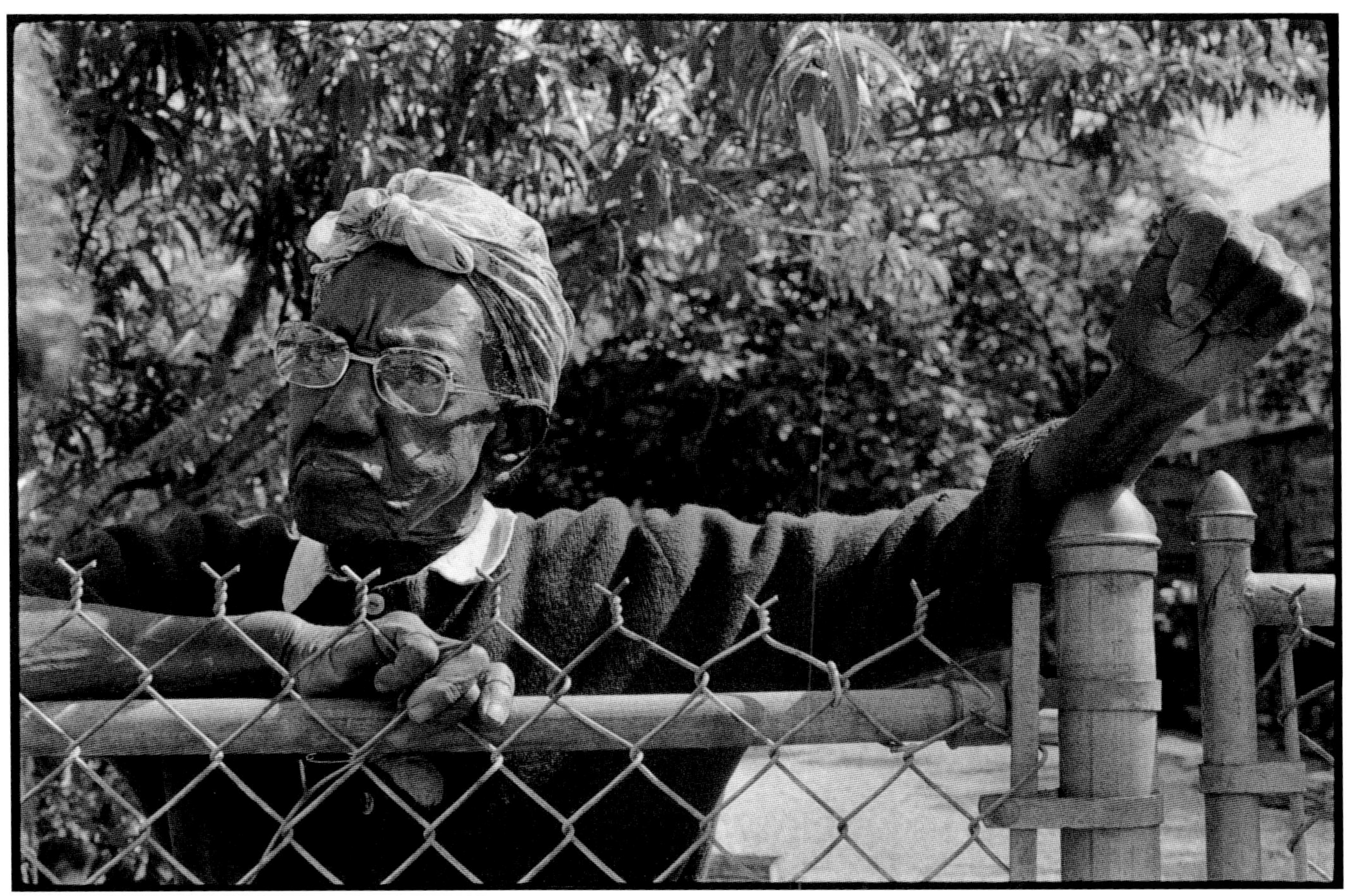

Fortitude, 1982
New Orleans, LA

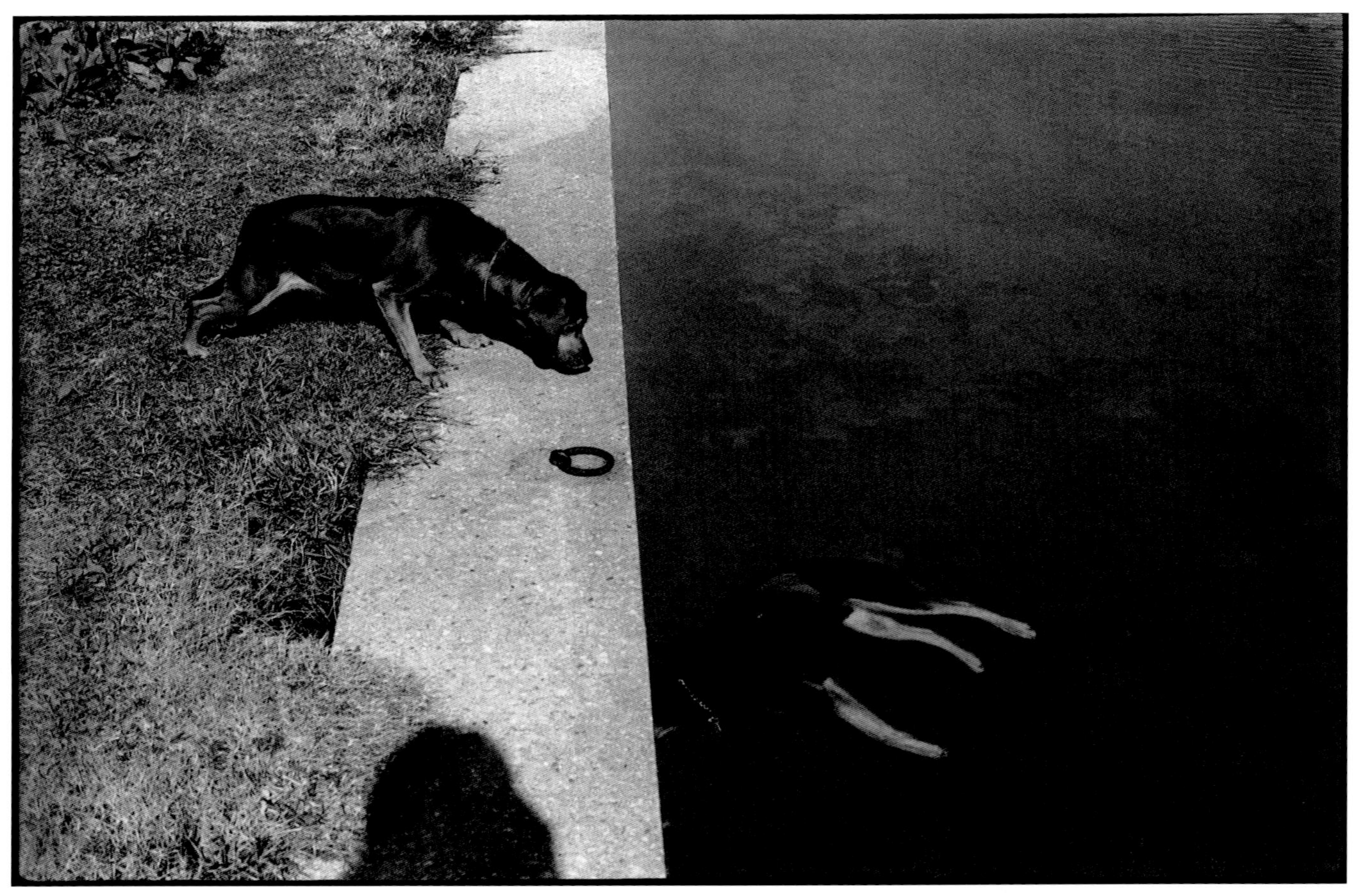

Argos - Death and Dogs, 1978
New Orleans, LA

Heart and Grave, 1994
New Orleans, LA

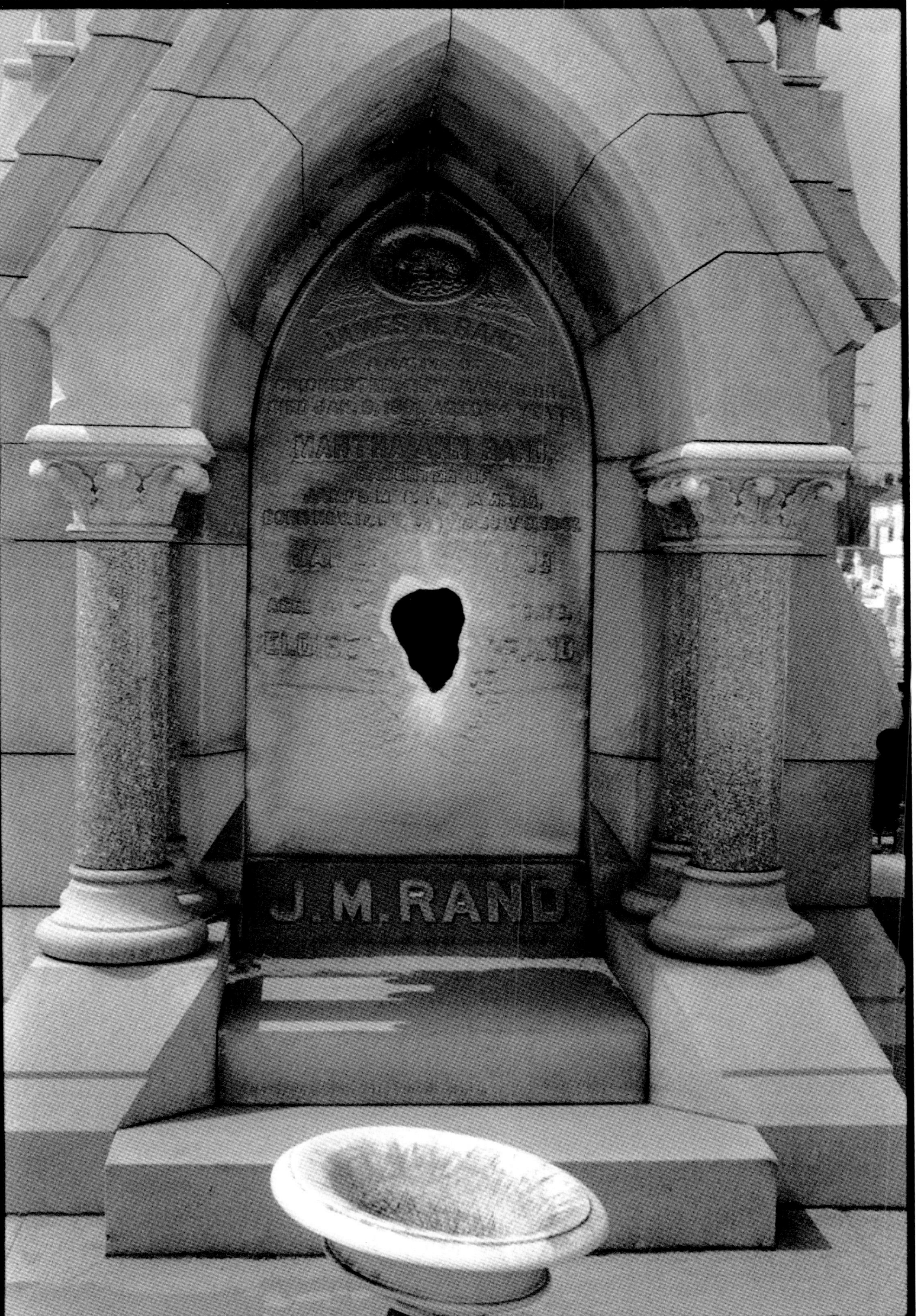

JAMES M. RAND,
A NATIVE OF
CHICHESTER, NEW HAMPSHIRE,
DIED JAN. 8, 1891, AGED 64 YEARS.
MARTHA ANN RAND,
DAUGHTER OF
JAMES M. & M. A. RAND,
BORN NOV. 12, 18__ DIED JULY 8, 1842.
JA
AGED
ELOISE RAND,
J. M. RAND

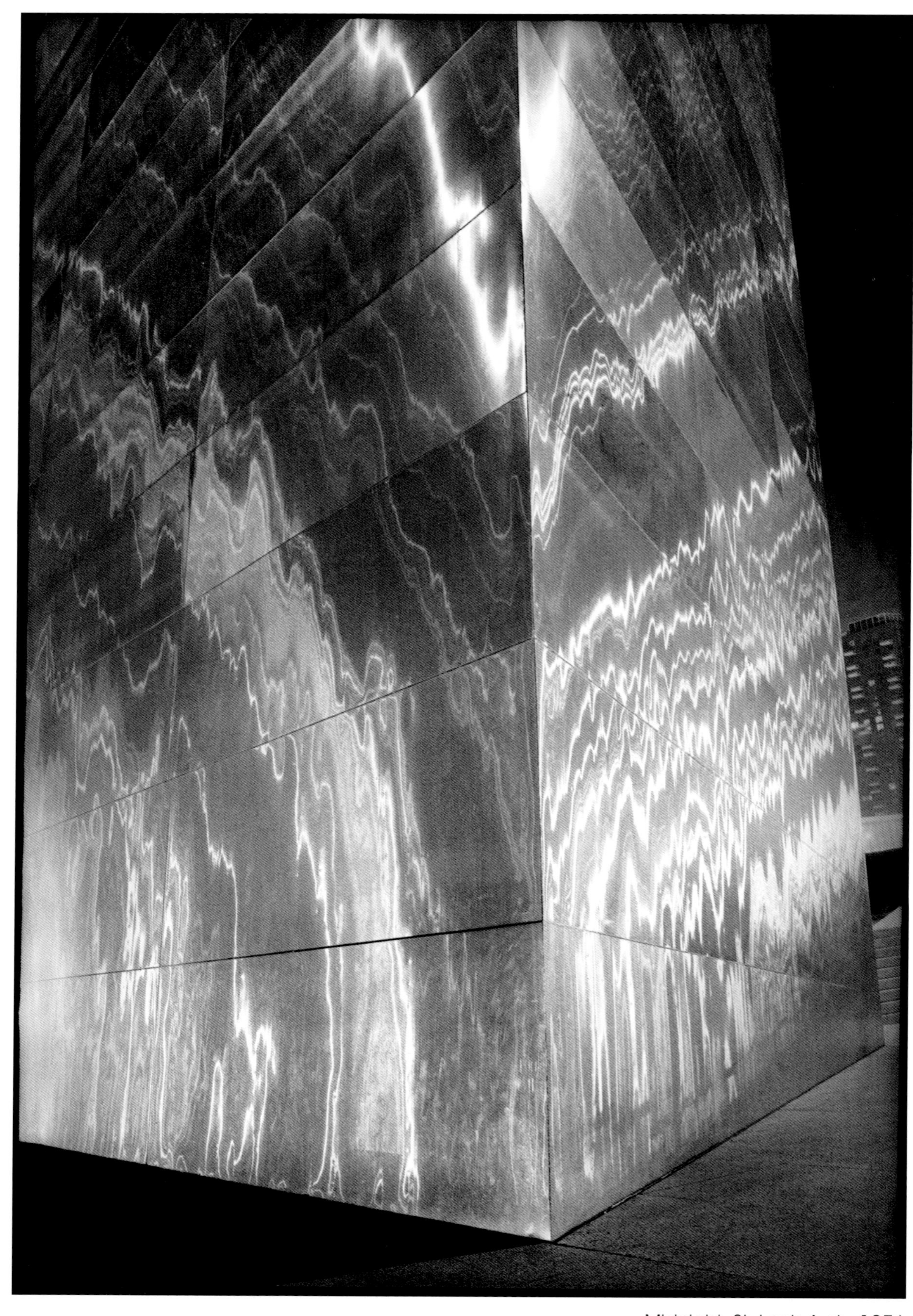

Midnight, St. Louis Arch, 1976
St. Louis, MO

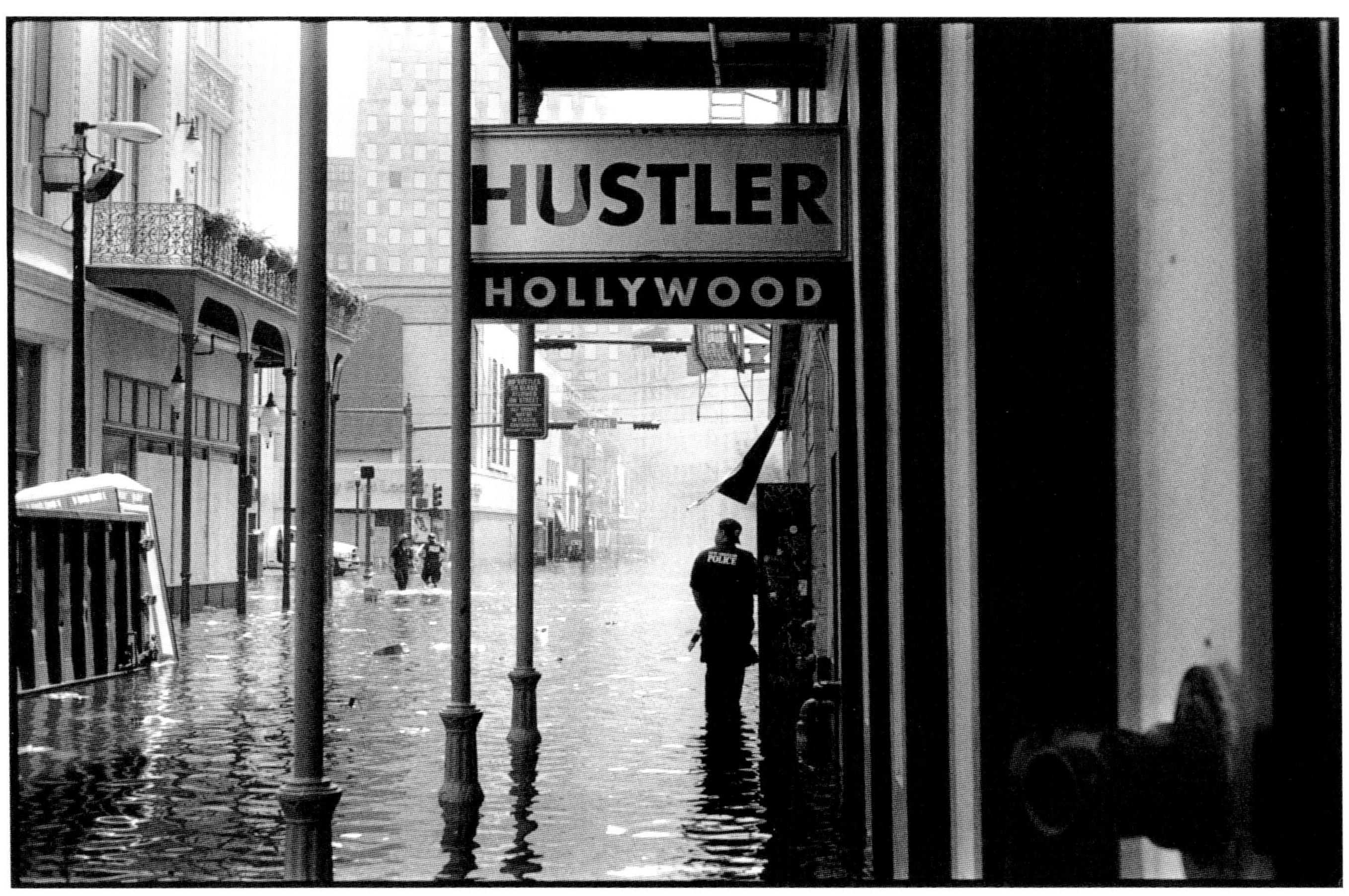

Hustler Hollywood, 2005
New Orleans, LA.

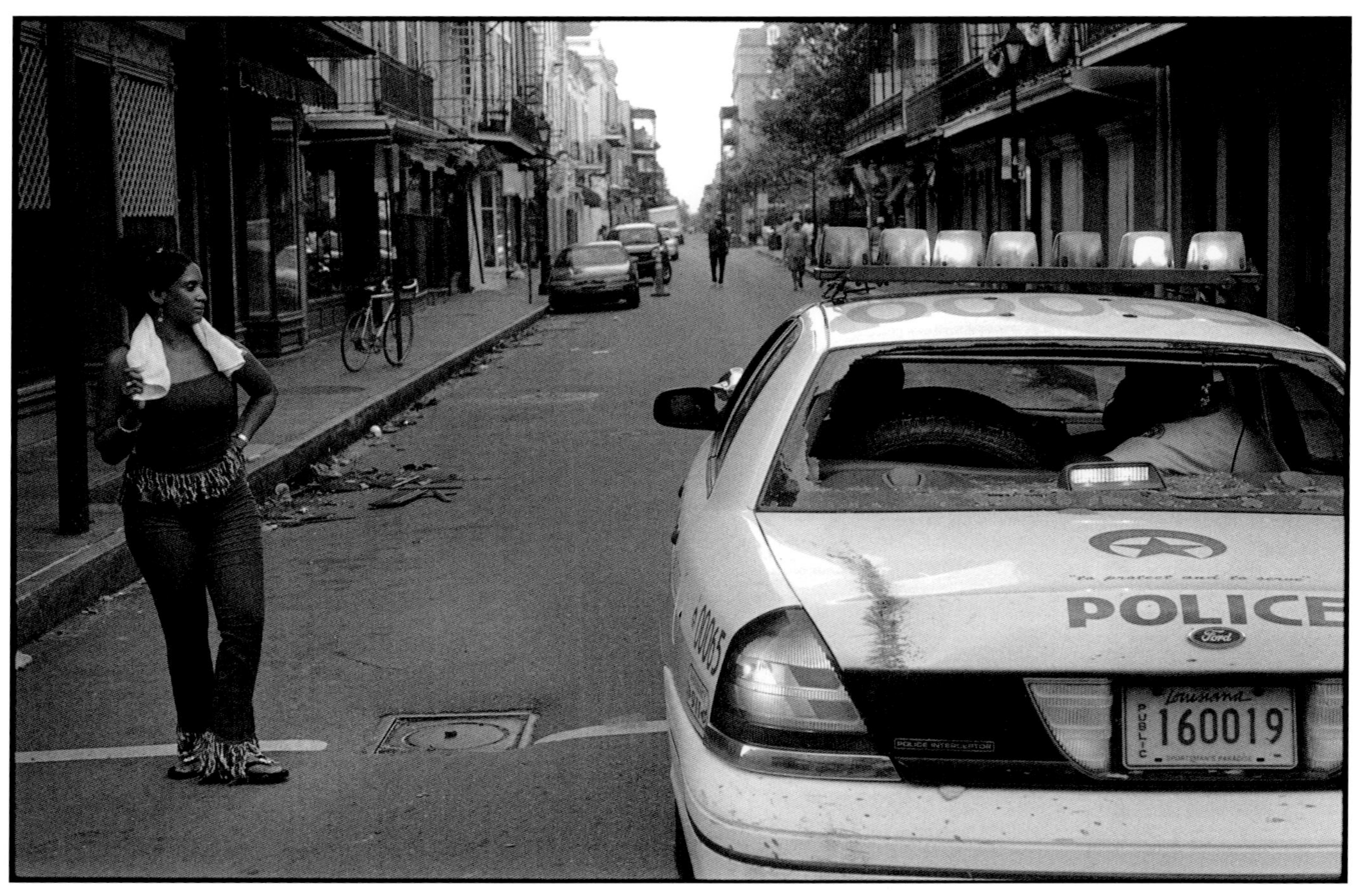

Wrong Way, 2005
New Orleans, LA

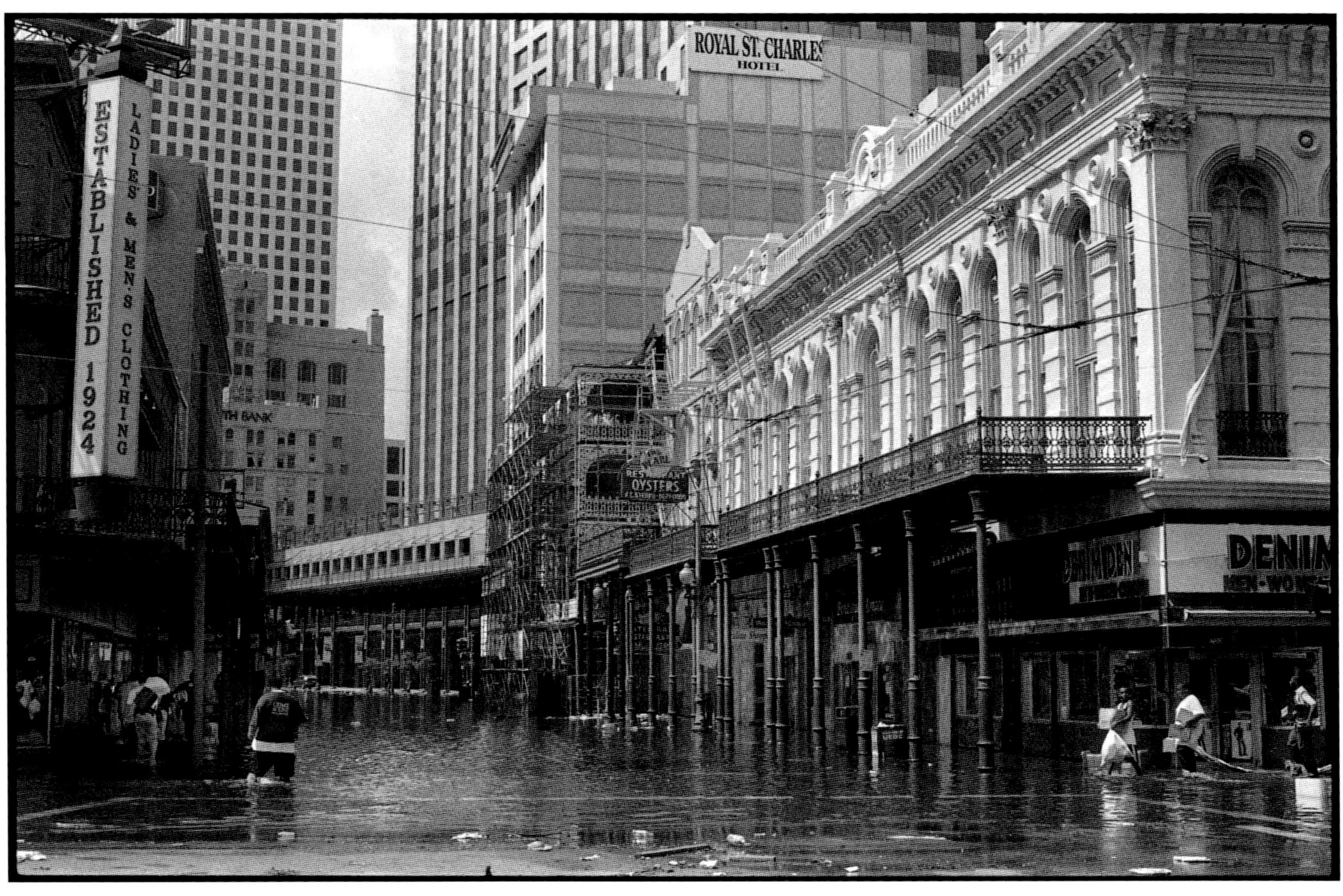

Crime Scene, 2005
New Orleans, LA

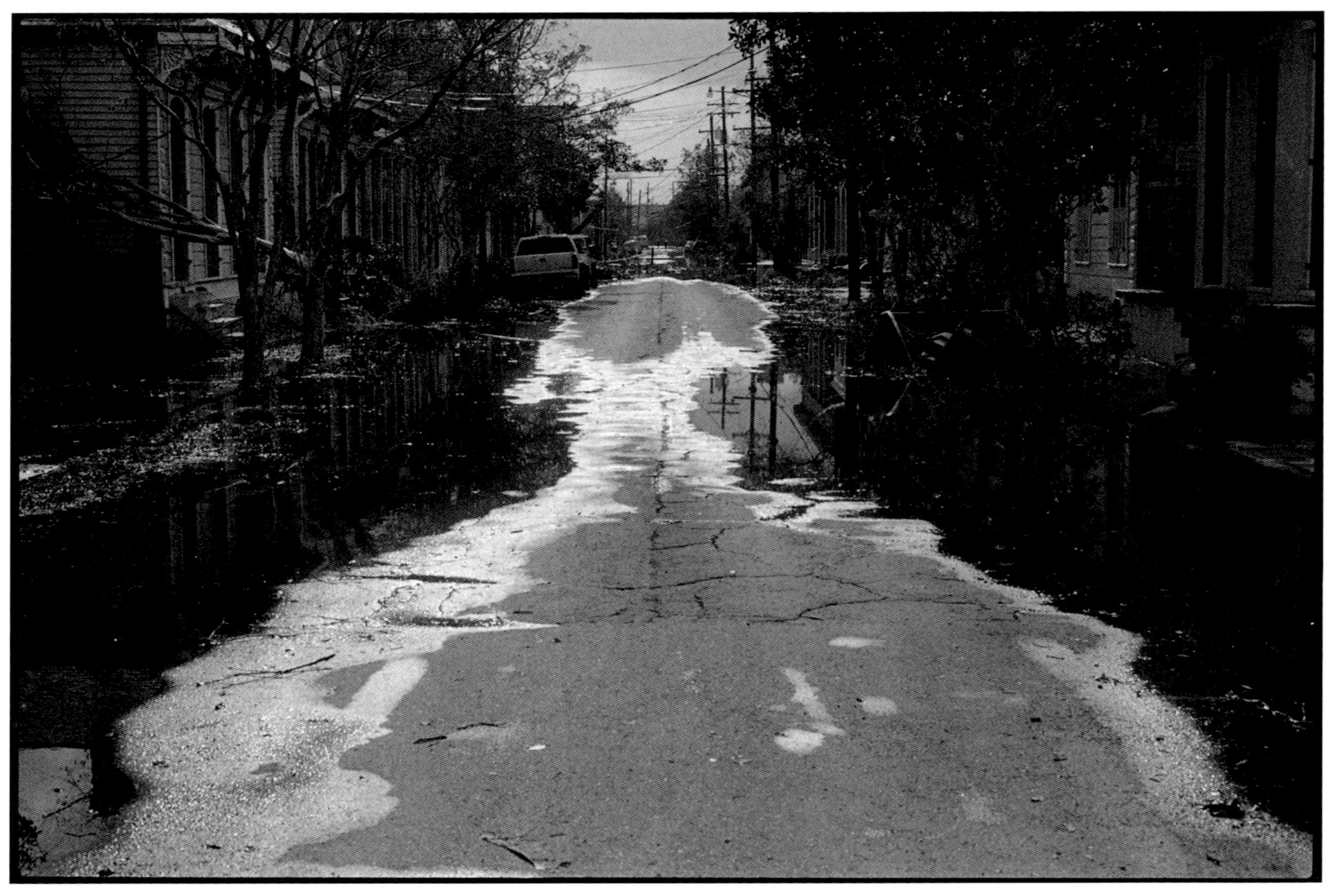

The Edge of the Federal Flood, 2005
New Orleans, LA

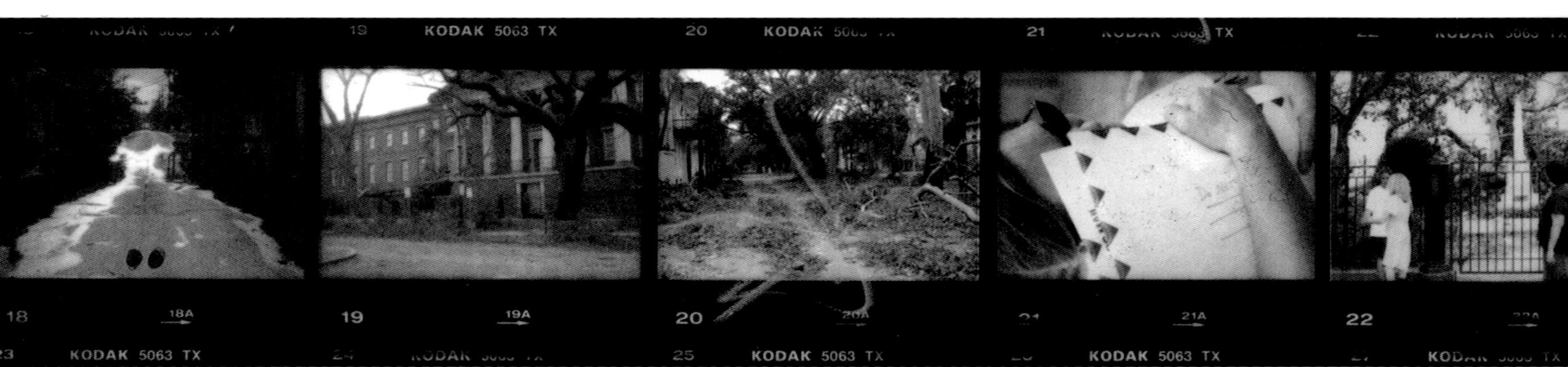

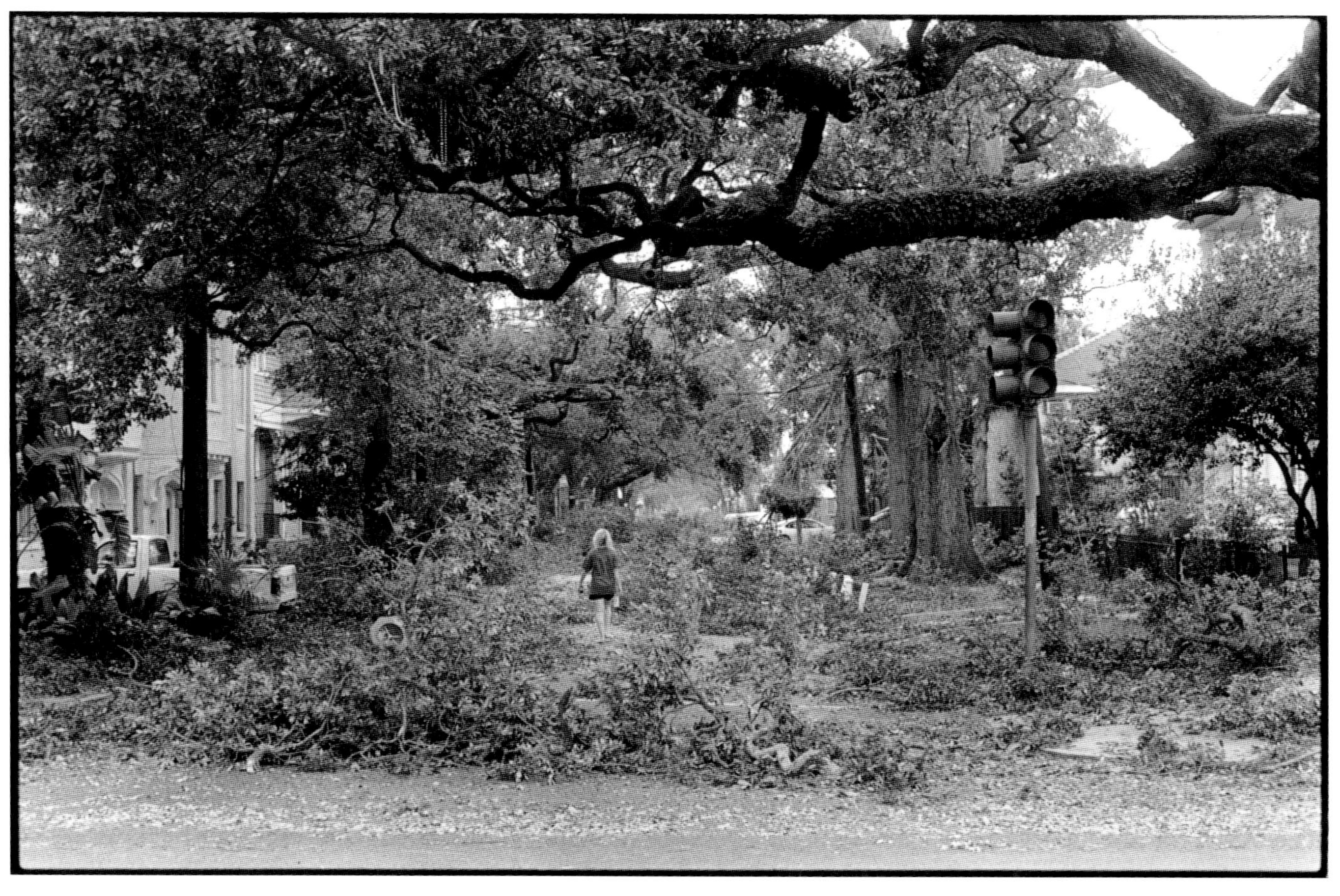

Wonderland, 2005
New Orleans, LA

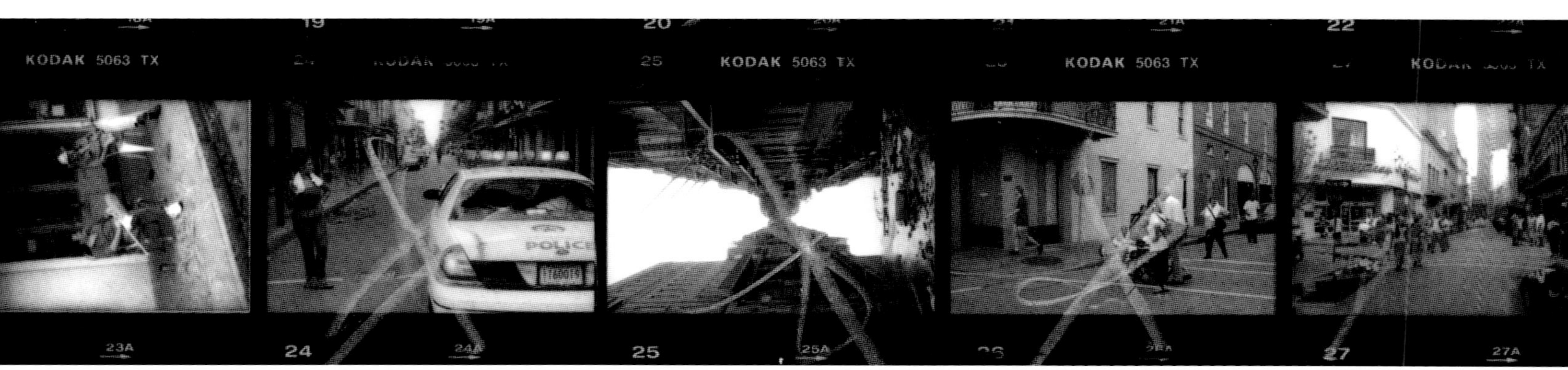

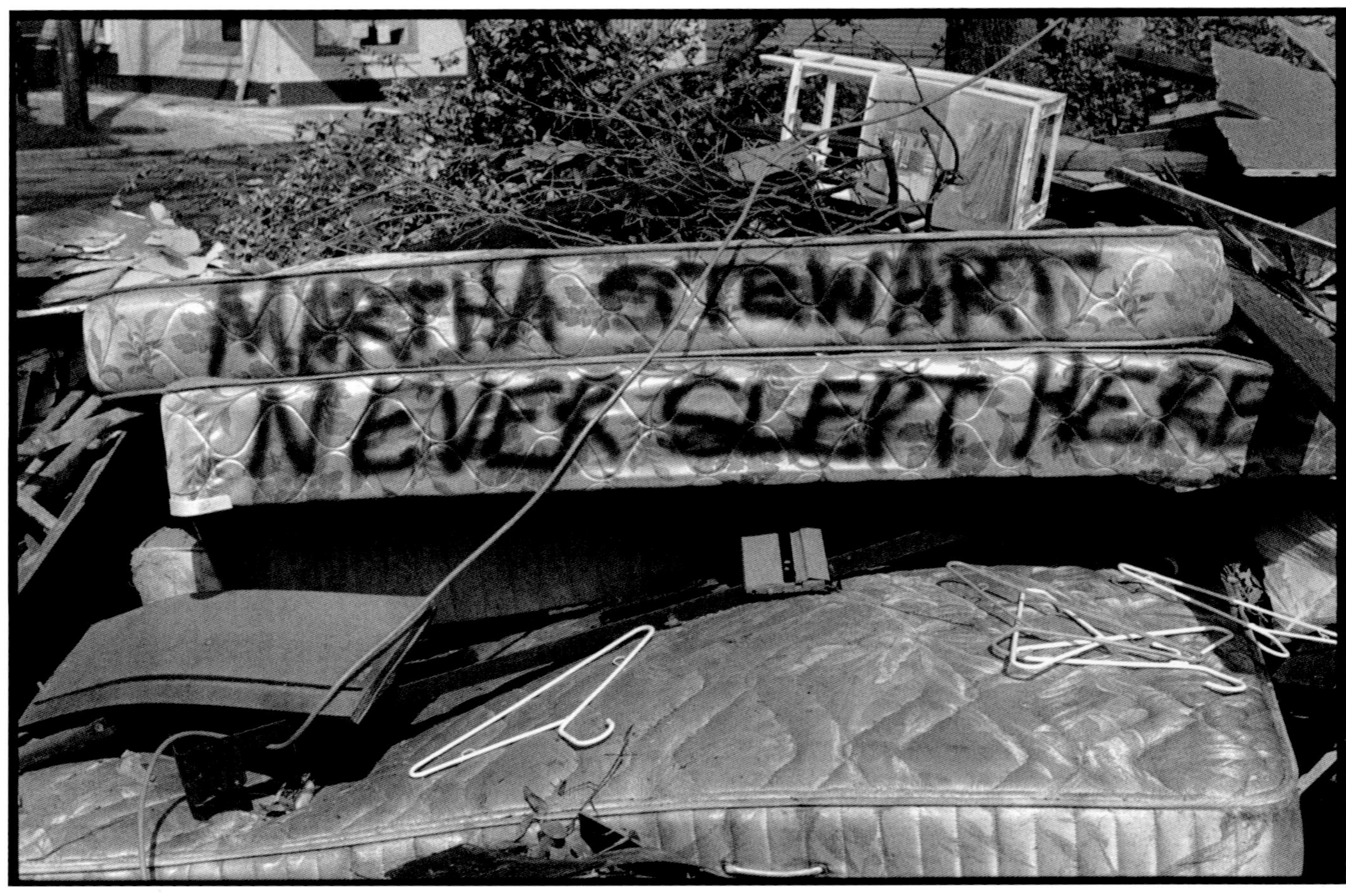

Martha Stewart Never Slept Here, 2005
New Orleans, LA

Imagine It Clean, 2005
New Orleans, LA

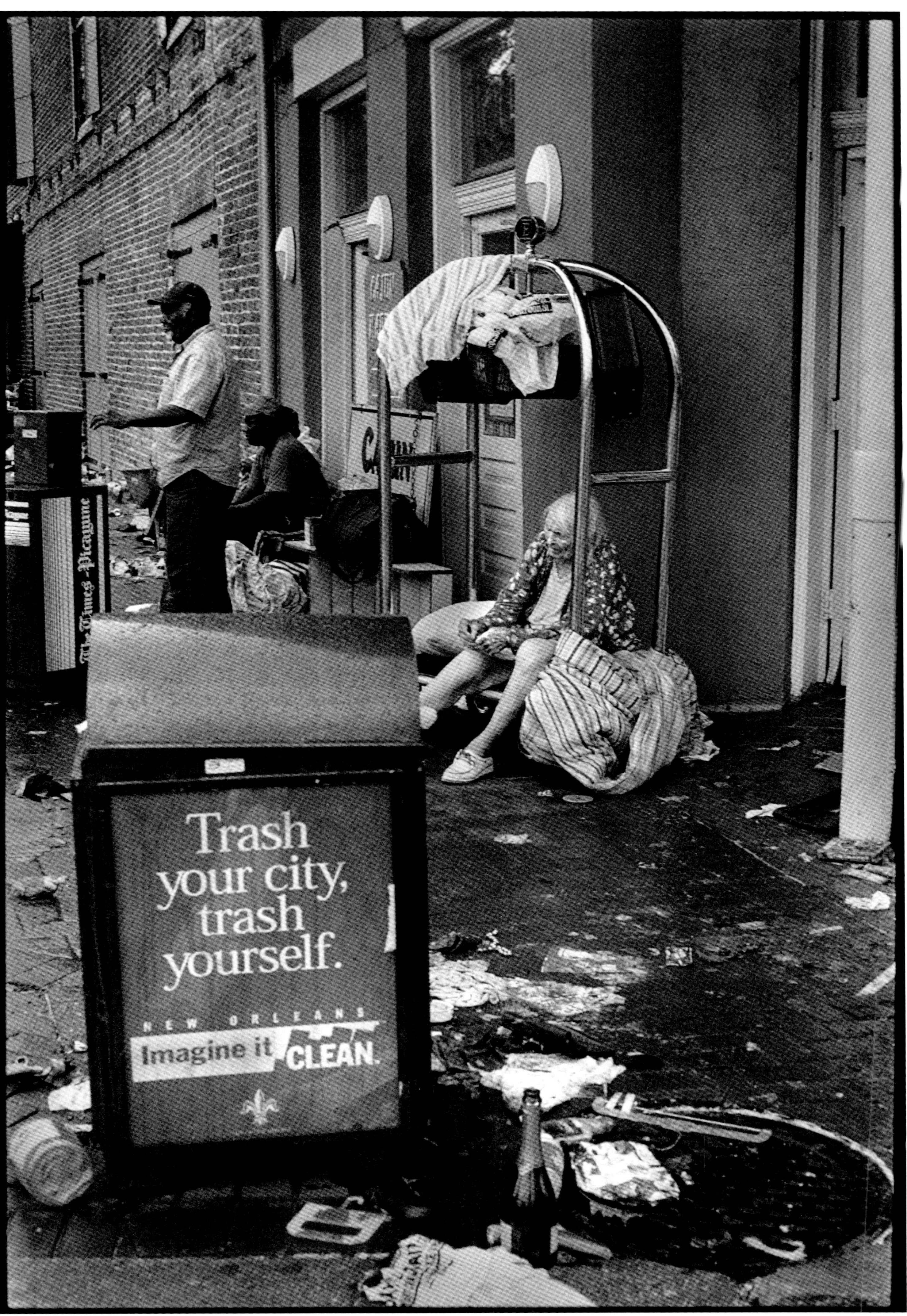
Trash
your city,
trash
yourself.
NEW ORLEANS
Imagine it CLEAN.

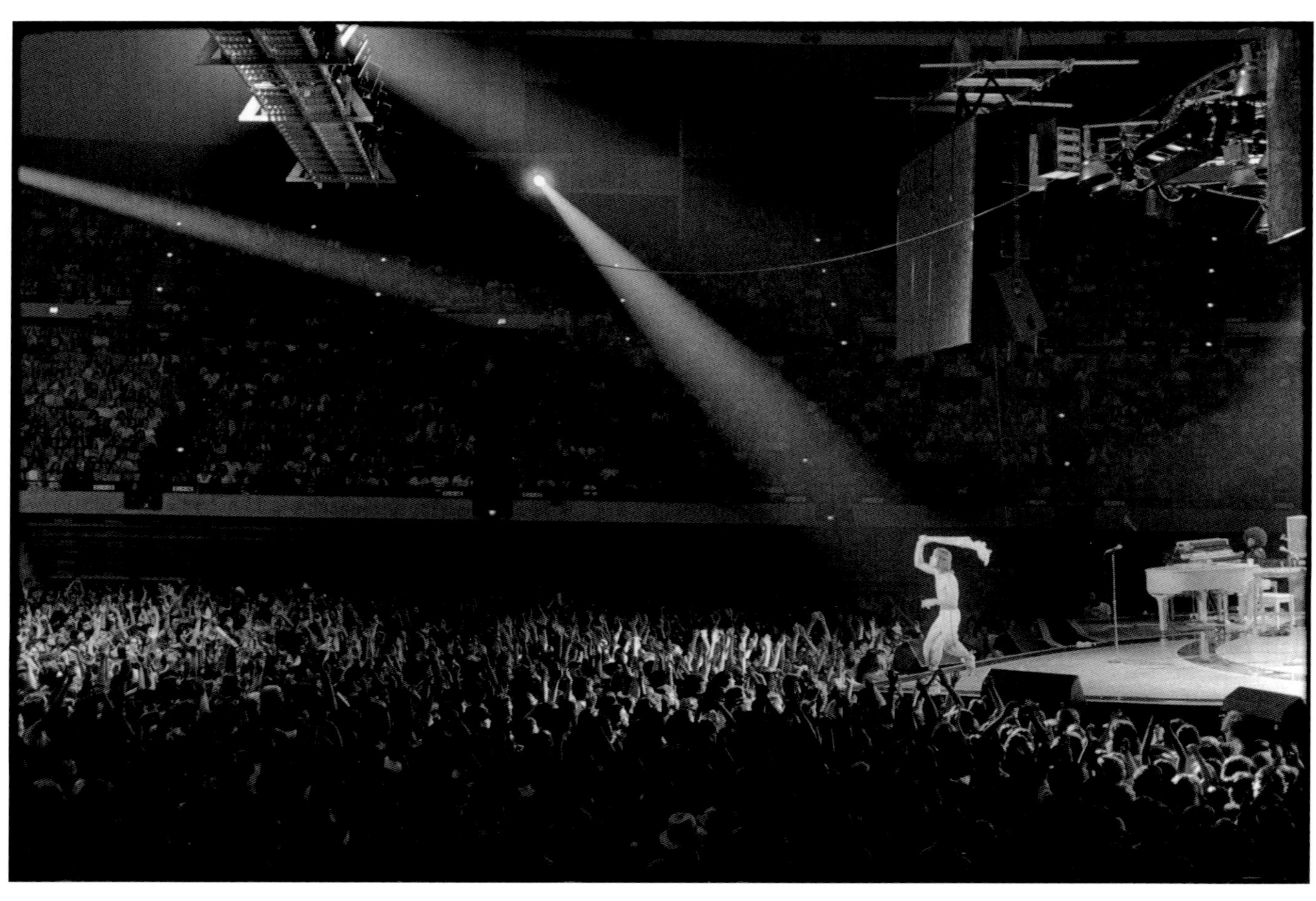

Rolling Stones, Mick Jagger and Billy Preston, 1975
Baton Rouge, LA

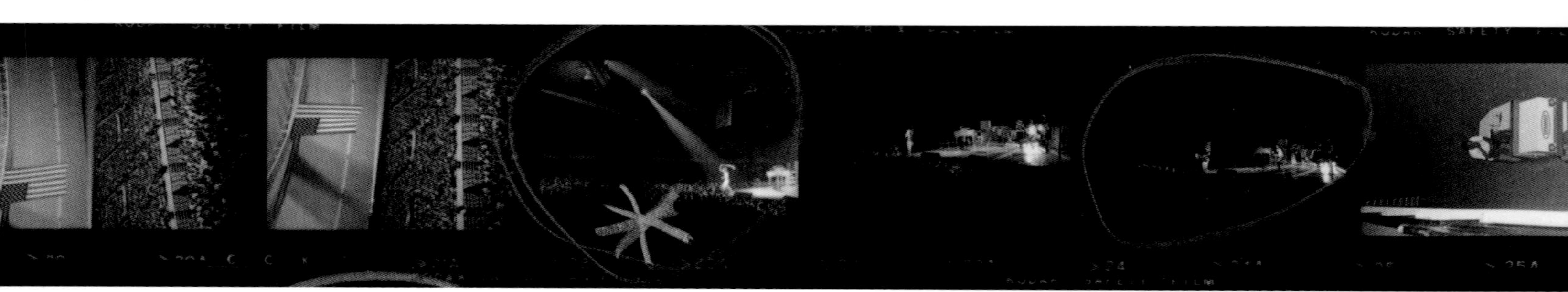

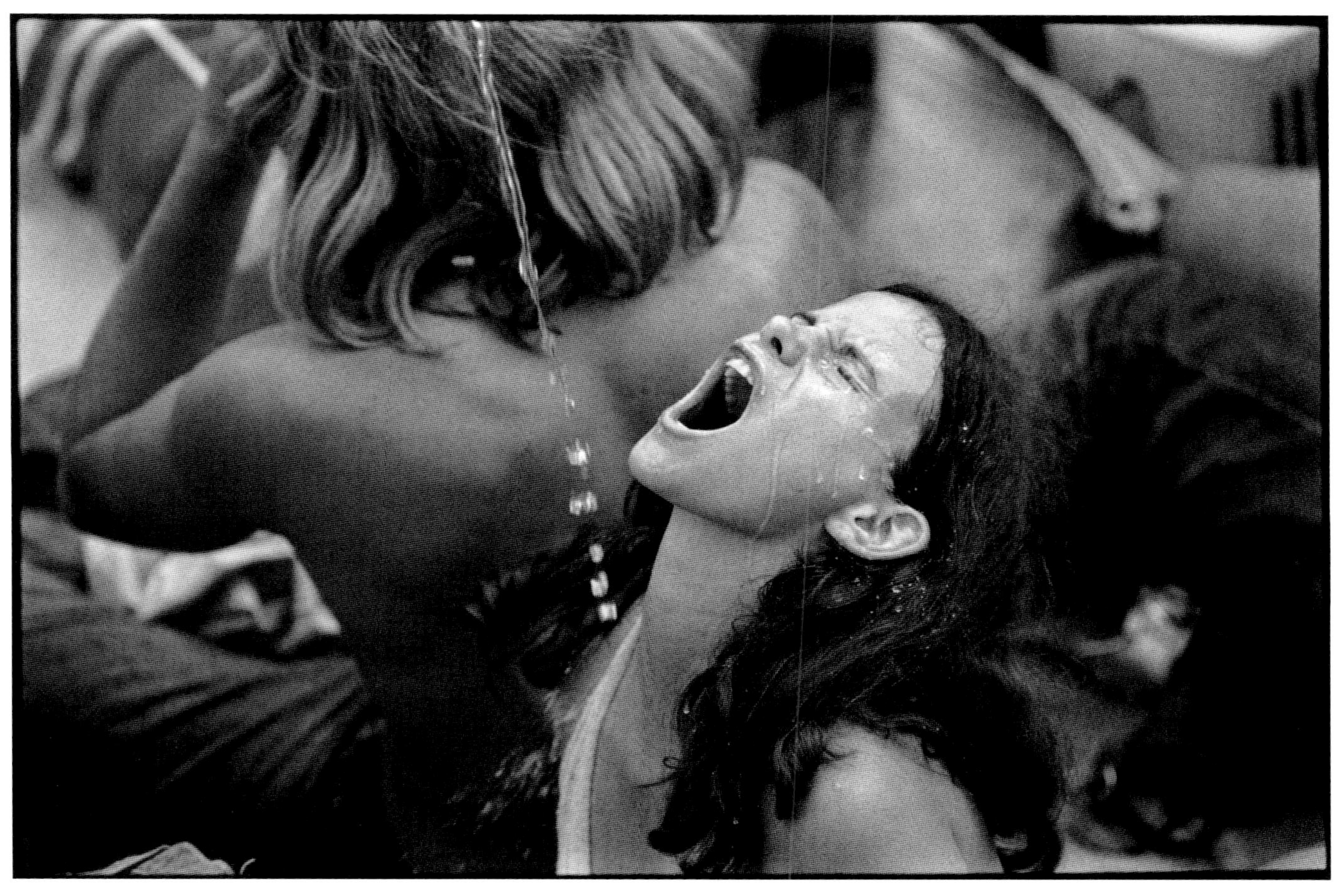

Wet, 1975
Dallas, TX

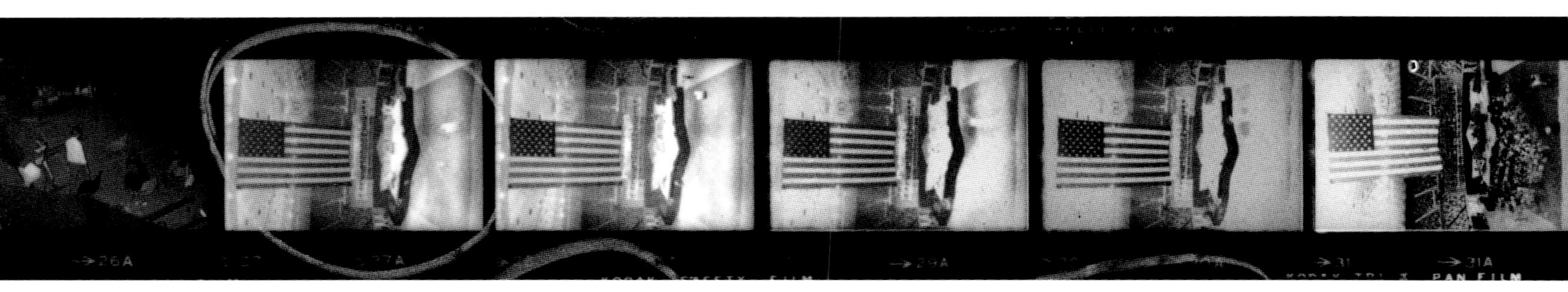

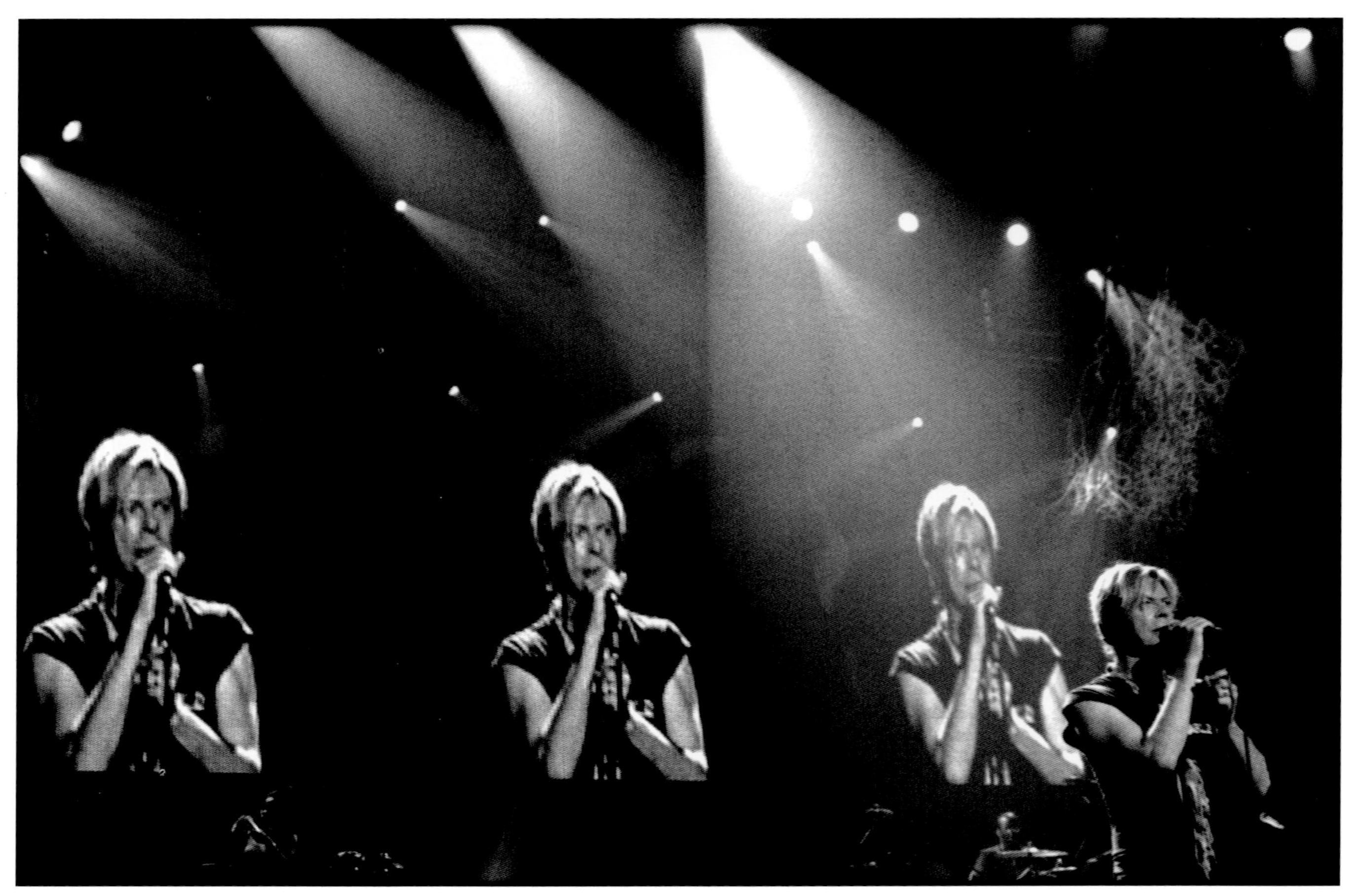

David Bowie, 2004
New Orleans, LA

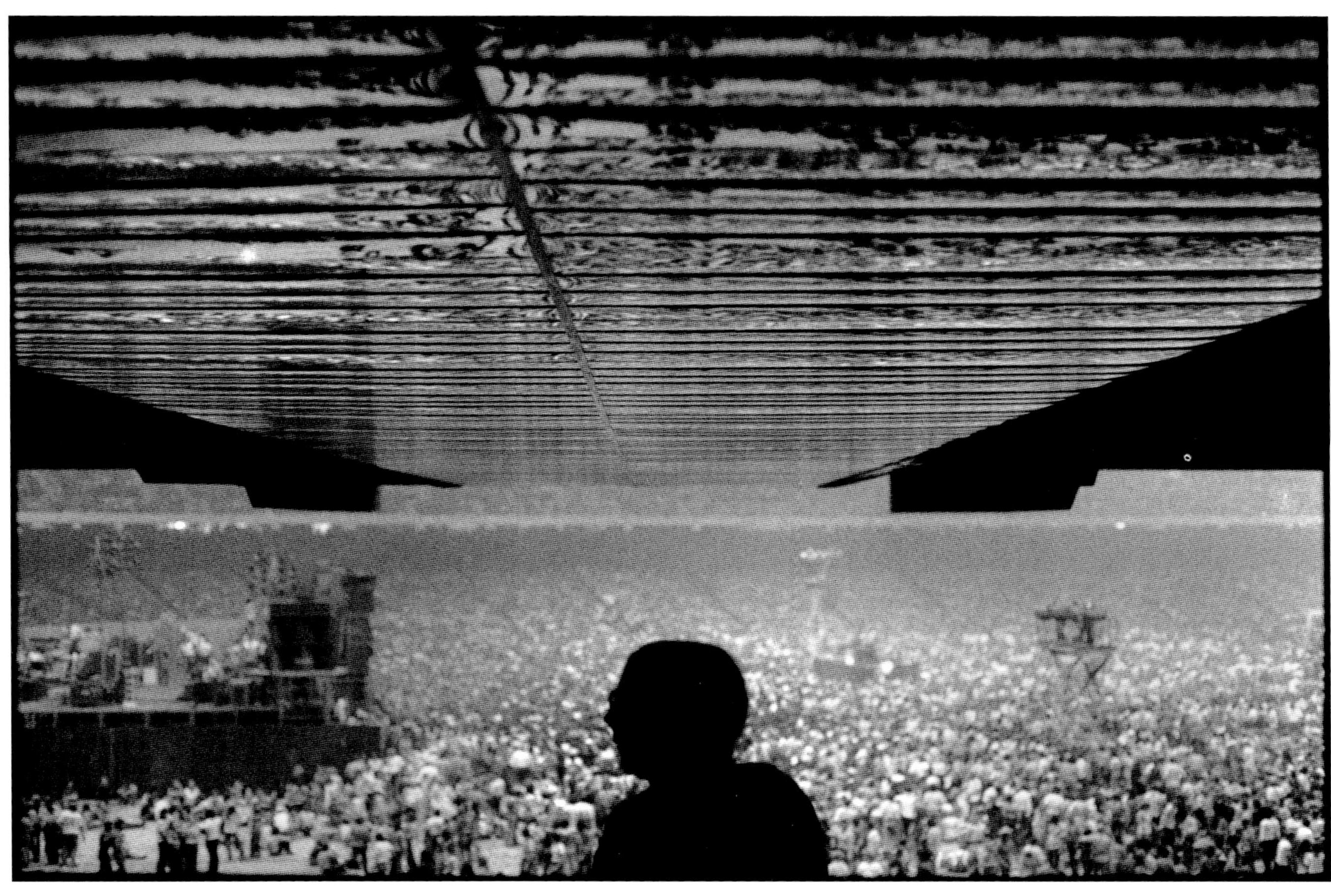

Superdome Sea, 1975
New Orleans, LA

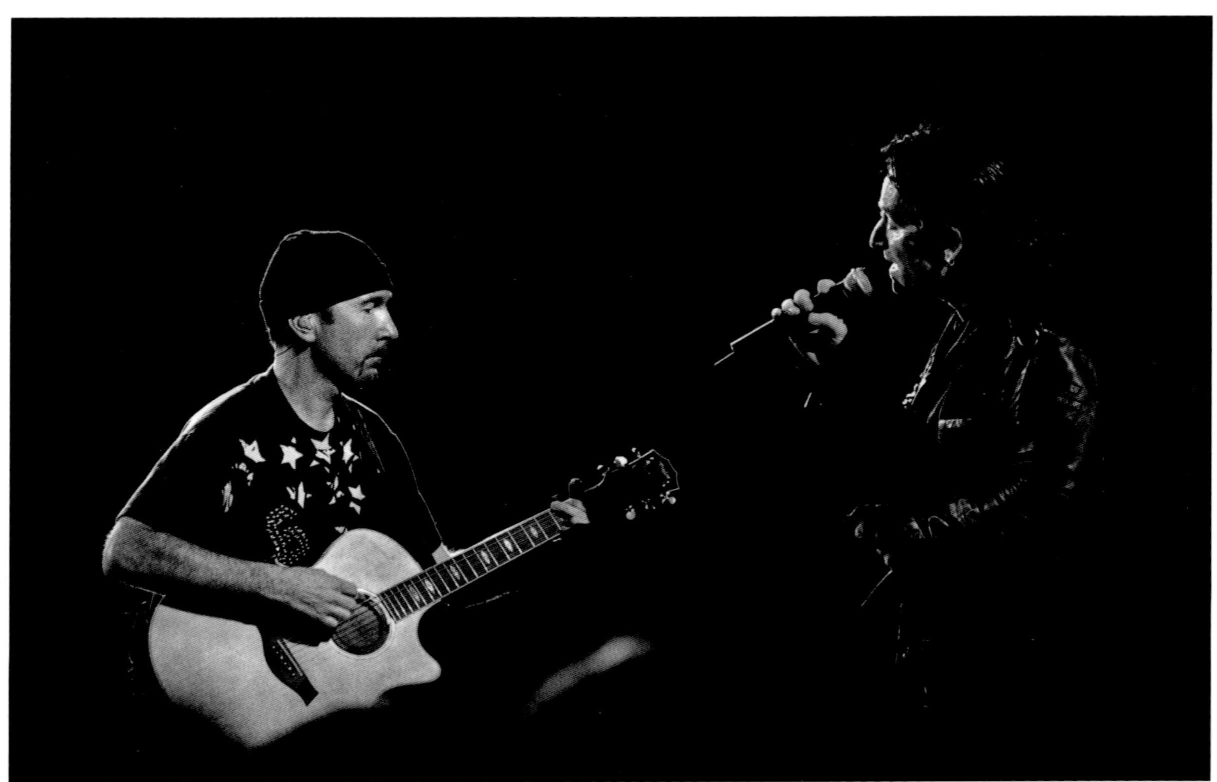

Words and Chords, Edge and Bono, 2001
Austin, TX

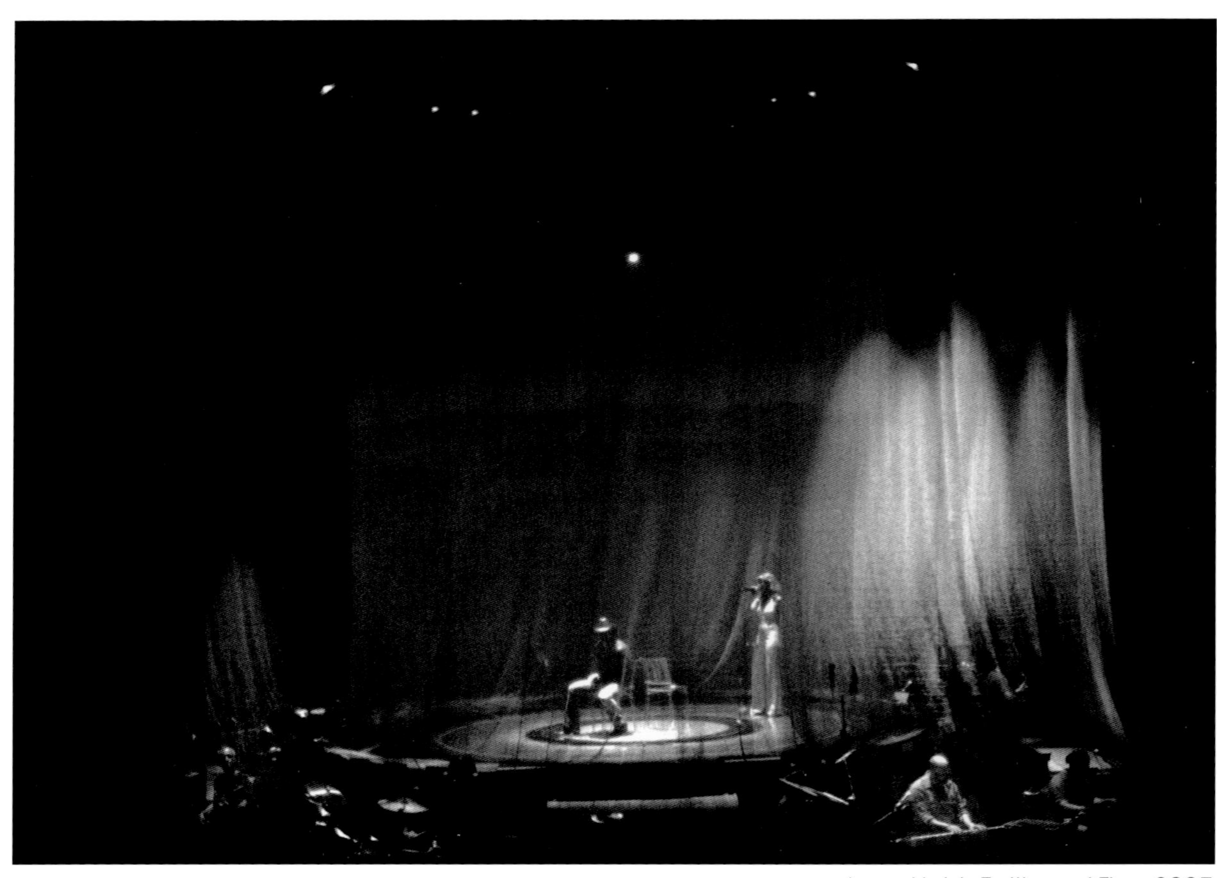

Love Light, Faith and Tim, 2007
Biloxi, MS

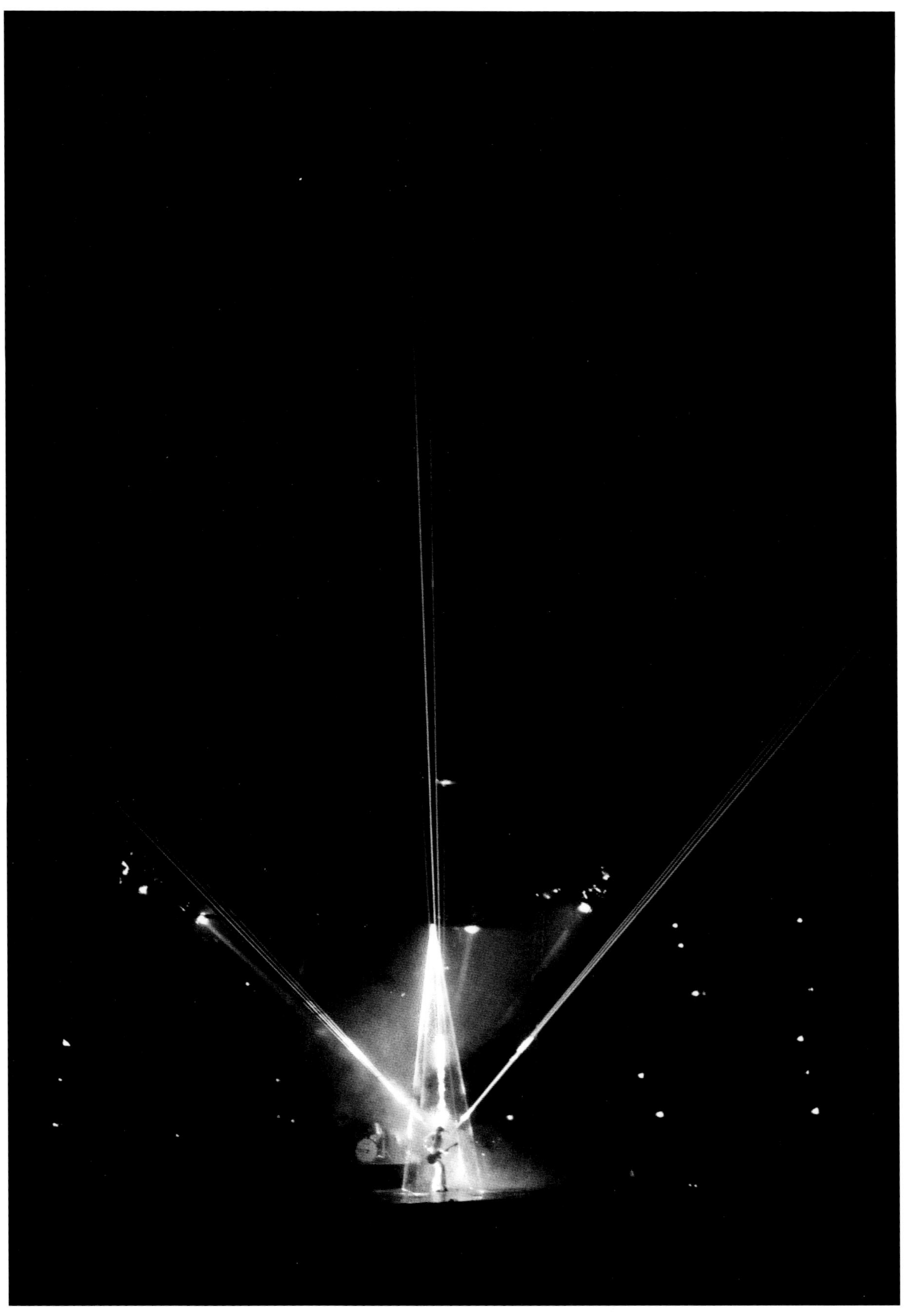

Electric Guitar Light, Jimmy Page, Led Zeppelin, 1975
Baton Rouge, LA

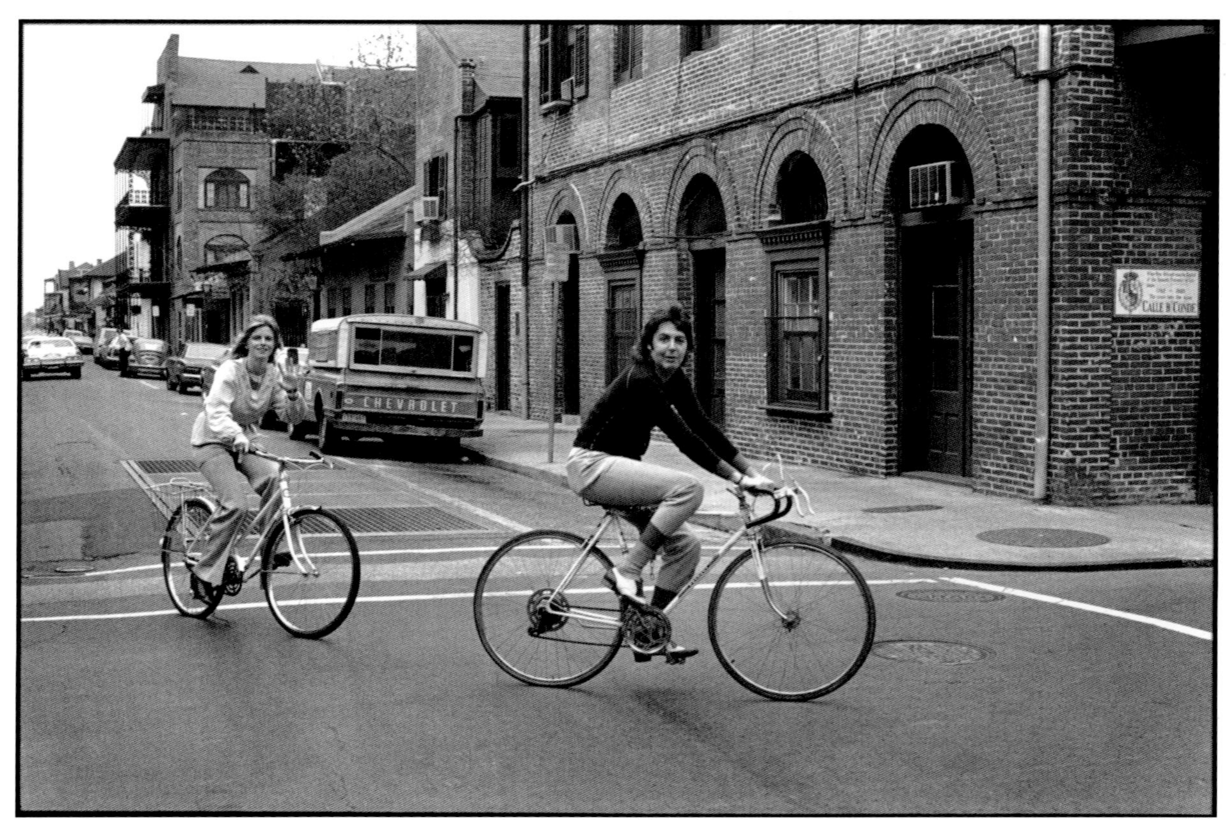

Venus and Mars, 1975
New Orleans, LA

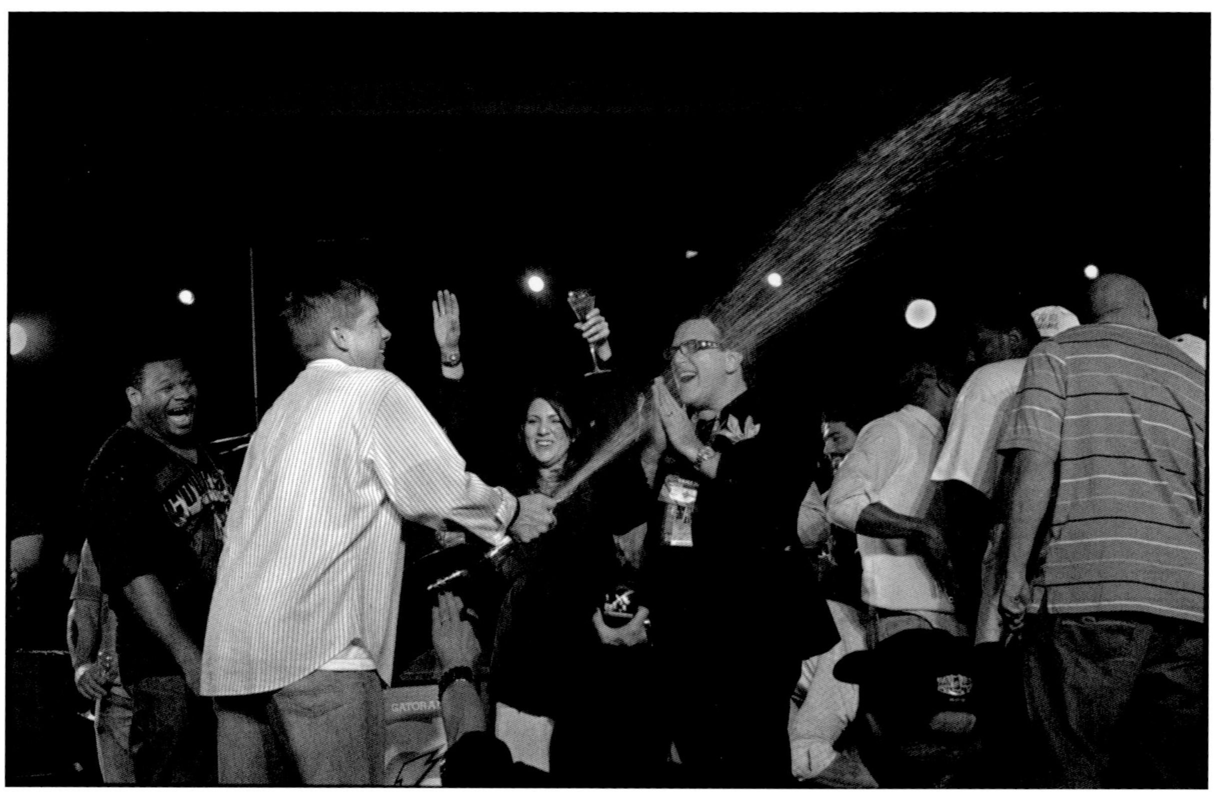

World Champions Champagne, 2010
Miami, FL

BIOGRAPHY

Joshua Mann Pailet is a documentary photographer known for capturing once in a lifetime moments and events. Born in 1950 in New Orleans, he moved to Baton Rouge at the age of two. His mother, Charlotte Mann Pailet, led his creative journey through reading and encouraging childhood interests. Their biweekly visits to the public library offered the opportunity to discover the magic of stereographs, Pailet's introduction to the world of photography.

In the early 1970s, Pailet was on a path to an engineering/business/economics career while attending Rice University. Fortunately, the photographer and teacher, Eve Sonneman, guided his interest in photography. During this time, Pailet installed his first photography exhibition and met Dominique and John de Menil, of the Menil Foundation. They purchased a selection of his photographs and further encouraged his lifelong passion for photography. Pailet graduated from Rice University with a B.A. in Economics and a B.S. in Business.

Joshua Mann Pailet's passion for photography led to the opening of A Gallery For Fine Photography in 1973. At a time when photography was fighting for legitimacy in the fine art world, A Gallery opened as one of the world's first art galleries to specialize in fine art photography. In 1975, A Gallery for Fine Photography premiered a solo exhibition with one of the great masters of photography, Ansel Adams. Today, A Gallery displays 19th, 20th and 21st century gems that rank with any museum collection.

Pailet's Archive includes ordinary Americans, musicians, artists, and actors who captivated his heart. His photographs are a treasure of Americana with highlights including historic events like the aftermath of Hurricane Katrina in New Orleans and the American Freedom Train tour of 1976. Joshua Mann Pailet lives in New Orleans, continues to photograph the world, and believes the best is yet to come.

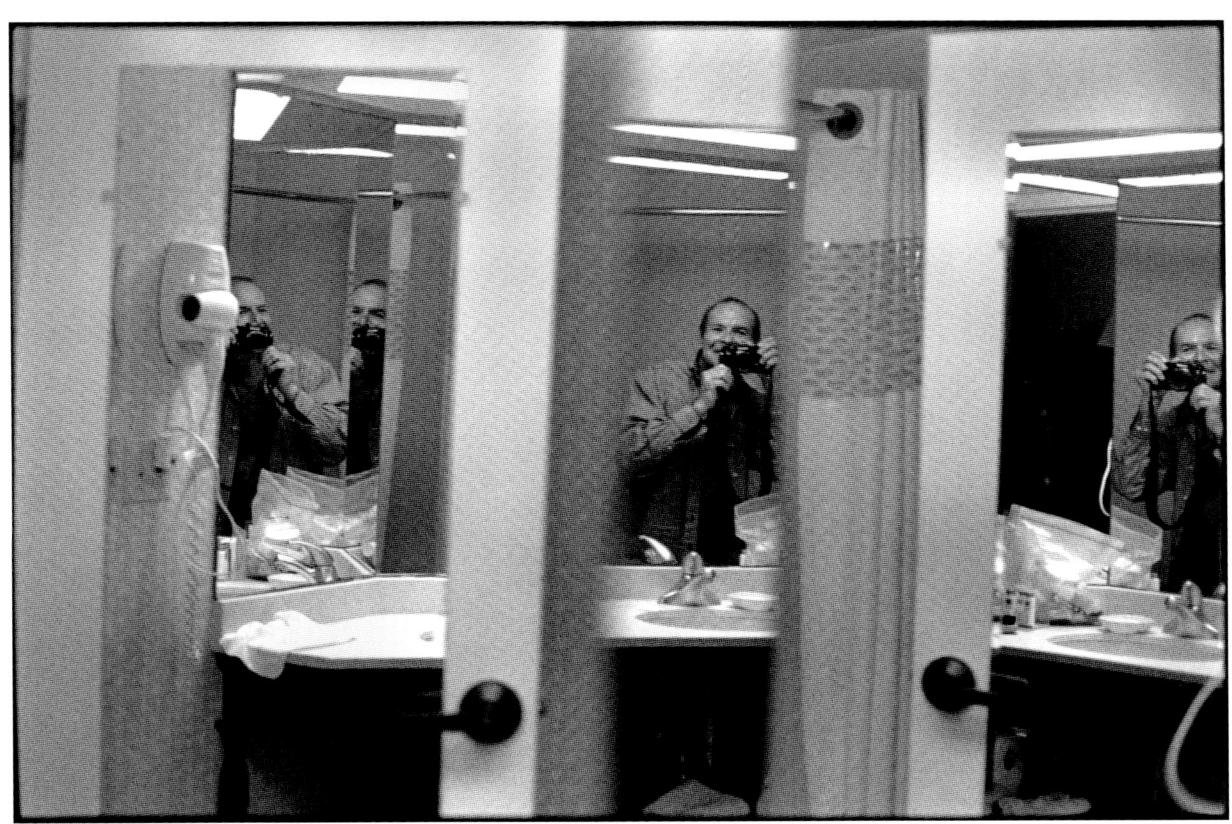

The Terrace Self-Portrait, 2008
Lakeland, FL

ACKNOWLEDGEMENTS

by Joshua Mann Pailet, A Gallery for Fine Photography, www.agallery.com

The editing and presentation of my Archive has been a prime focus since Hurricane Katrina. As I photographed in the days and weeks after the Storm, the blessing of collaboration unfolded. With the darkroom talent of David Zietz in Baton Rouge and the generous help of Richard Colton, I was able to establish my archive enterprise and production of exhibition silver gelatin photographs. This activity required the teamwork of many people including Edward Hebert, Jenny Bagert, and Celeste Marshall.

Since October 2005, we have produced, cataloged, and edited over 5,000 8"x10" photographs as a Master Archive Set. Over 250 16"x20" photographs in sets of two or three were produced in preparation for this exhibit. The oversized (36"x56") photographs are my first adventure with digital printmaking.

My thanks to Director Dan Stetson and Curator Adam Justice at Polk Museum of Art, whose experienced eyes influenced the editing. My deepest appreciation goes to Robert Puterbaugh. His astute insights and generous support as a collector and friend is an inspiration.

Collections

The Menil Collection, Houston, TX
Bibliothèque Nationale de France, Paris, France
Louisiana Arts and Science Center, Baton Rouge, LA
New Orleans Museum of Art, New Orleans, LA
Smithsonian National Museum of American History, Washington, DC
Wallis Annenberg and the Annenberg Foundation, Los Angeles, CA
Polk Museum of Art, Lakeland, FL
The Richard Colton Collection, New Orleans, LA
The Cherye R. and James F. Pierce Collection, Honolulu, HI
The Robert & Malena Puterbaugh Collection, Lakeland, FL

Exhibitions

Joshua Mann Pailet and Scott Michael Coburn, Mardi Gras, Rice University, Houston, TX, 1972
New Orleans Mardi Gras, A Gallery For Fine Photography, New Orleans, LA, 1975
Louisiana Artworks '84, The World's Fair, New Orleans, LA, 1984
The World's Fair, New Orleans, A Gallery for Fine Photography, New Orleans, LA, 1987
Everyday People: 20th Century Photography, The Menil Museum, Houston, TX, 2005
Katrina Exposed, New Orleans Museum of Art, New Orleans, LA, 2006
Eye of the Storm, I Witness, Architrouve Gallery, Chicago, IL, 2006
Eye See America: Through the Lens of Joshua Mann Pailet, Polk Museum of Art, Lakeland, FL, 2010

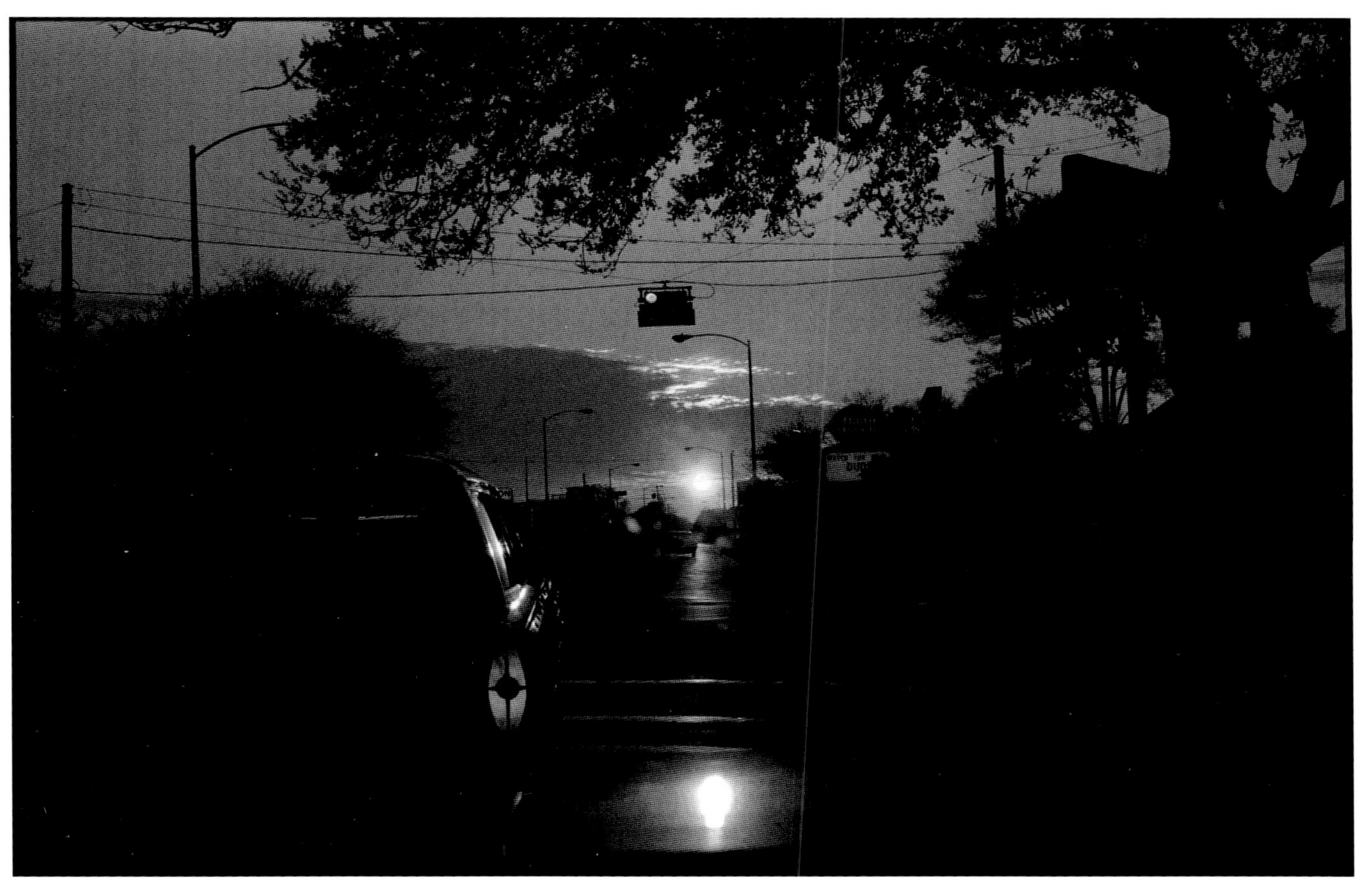

On the Road, 1976
Galveston, TX

EXHIBITION CHECKLIST

All photographs by Joshua Mann Pailet, and lent Courtesy of the Artist unless otherwise noted. The exhibition consists of 16"x20" and 11"x14" silver gelatin prints and 36"x56" archival pigment prints on paper.

1. *Self-Portrait, Houston, TX,* 1971 (p.11)

2. *Handshake Tracks, New Orleans, LA,* 1974 (p.16)

3. *Man and Apes, New Orleans, LA,* 1974 (p.51)
Collection of Polk Museum of Art
Gift of Robert and Malena Puterbaugh

4. *Don't Ask Me, Baton Rouge, LA,* 1974 (p.52)
Collection of Robert and Malena Puterbaugh

5. *Chinese News, San Francisco, CA,* 1974 (p.25)

6. *Apartments, Pipes, and Sports, San Francisco, CA,* 1974 (p.15)

7. *Nixon Loses Tapes, San Francisco, CA,* 1975 (p.27)

8. *Topless, San Francisco, CA,* 1974 (p.24)

9. *Superdome Sea, New Orleans, LA,* 1975 (p.67)
Digital pigment print

10. *Rolling Stones, Mick Jagger and Billy Preston, Baton Rouge, LA,* 1975 (p.64)

11. *Wet, Dallas, TX,* 1975 (p.65)

12. *Electric Guitar Light, Jimmy Page, Led Zeppelin, Baton Rouge, LA,* 1975 (p.69)

13. *Venus & Mars, New Orleans, LA,* 1975 (p.70)

14. *The Mayfair Flirt, Scranton, PA,* 1976 (p.19)
Collection of Robert and Malena Puterbaugh

15. *Center Street, Scranton, PA,* 1976 (p.20)
Digital pigment print

16. *Diamond Lust, New York, NY,* 1976 (p.31)

17. *The 4449, American Freedom Train, Jacksonville, FL,* 1976 (p.13)

18. *Club House Construction, Tulsa, OK,* 1976 (p.14)

19. *Midnight, St. Louis Arch, St. Louis, MO,* 1976 (p.56)
Digital pigment print

20. *Haute Couture/Magic Copy, Scranton, PA,* 1976 (p.18)

21. *Long Live Freedom, Kansas,* 1976 (p.12)
Digital pigment print

22. *Beneficial Finance System, Cumberland, MD,* 1976 (p.21)

23. *American Workers, Pennsylvania,* 1976 (p.17)

24. *On the Road, Galveston, TX,* 1976 (p.73)

25. *Company, Inc., New Orleans, LA,* 1977 (p.50)

26. *Argos - Death and Dogs, New Orleans, LA,* 1978 (p.54)

27. *Guard Teaching Art, The National Gallery, Washington, DC,* 1978 (p.38)

28. *All Conversions Approximate, New York, NY,* 1978 (p.43)
Collection of Robert and Malena Puterbaugh

29. *The Mall, Atlanta, GA,* 1979 (p.37)

30. *InElegant Cigarette, Washington, DC,* 1980 (p.36)
Collection of Lindsay Raley and Michelle Chandler-Raley

31. *Dream, New York, NY,* 1982 (p.22)

32. *Fortitude, New Orleans, LA,* 1982 (p.53)

33. *Greco's Grocery, Robert, LA,* 1983 (p.48)

34. *Shadow People, New Orleans, LA,* 1984 (p.41)

35. *Hell of a Joint, New York, NY,* 1984 (p.28)

36. *New York City, New York, NY,* 1988 (p.40)

37. *A Weakness for Gold, New York, NY,* 1989 (p.30)

38. *The Chat, New Orleans, LA,* 1989 (p.33)

39. *"Uncle" Lionel Batiste, New Orleans, LA,* 1990 (p.46)

40. *Journey to Eternity, Paris to Zurich,* 1990 (p.42)

41. *Frozen Love, New York, NY,* 1990 (p.39)
Collection of Robert and Joy Williams

42. *Tempo, New York, NY,* 1991 (p.23)

43. *Sam's Dog, Boudin, VA,* 1993 (p.4)

44. *Heart and Grave, New Orleans, LA,* 1994 (p.55)

45. *Pun Spa, New York, NY,* 1996 (p.29)

46. *Beam Me Up Scotty, St-Germain-des-Prés, Paris, France,* 1997 (p.32)

47. *Piano Keys, New York, NY,* 1998 (p.25)

48. *Every Day, Best Sex, Big Money, New York, NY,* 1998 (p.26)

49. *Hair, New Orleans, LA,* 2000 (p.48)

50. *Second Line, New Orleans, LA,* 2001 (p.45)

51. *Words and Chords, Edge and Bono, Austin, TX,* 2001 (p.68)

52. *Sounds of Music, New Orleans, LA,* 2001 (p.47)

53. *David Bowie, New Orleans, LA,* 2004 (p.66)

54. *Wonderland, New Orleans, LA,* 2005 (p.61)

55. *Martha Stewart Never Slept Here, New Orleans, LA,* 2005 (p.62)

56. *Imagine It Clean, New Orleans, LA,* 2005 (p.63)
Collection of Travis Puterbaugh

57. *Crime Scene, New Orleans, LA,* 2005 (p.59)
Collection of Travis Puterbaugh

58. *Hustler Hollywood, New Orleans, LA,
    2005* (p.57)
    Digital pigment print

59. *The Edge of the Federal Flood, New
    Orleans, LA,* 2005 (p.60)

60. *Wrong Way, New Orleans, LA,* 2005
    (p.58)

61. *"Mr. Okra" Arthur Robinson, New
    Orleans, LA,* 2006 (p.49)
    Digital pigment print

62. *The Blizzard, New York, NY,* 2006 (p.5)

63. *Love Light, Faith and Tim, Biloxi, MS,*
    2007 (p.68)

64. *The Terrace Self-Portrait, Lakeland, FL,*
    2008 (p.71)

65. *She Dances, New Orleans, LA,* 2009
    (p.6)

66. *Red Hawk, Mardi Gras Indian, New
    Orleans, LA,* 2009 (p.44)

67. *World Champions Champagne, Miami,
    FL,* 2010 (p.70)

68. *Mardi Gras, New Orleans, LA,* 2010
    (p.49)

Frontispiece: *Herman Leonard, New Orleans,
    LA,* 2001